Jungian Dream Interpretation

Marie-Louise von Franz, Honorary Patron

**Studies in Jungian Psychology
by Jungian Analysts**

Daryl Sharp, General Editor

Jungian
Dream
Interpretation

A Handbook of Theory and Practice

James A. Hall, M.D.

To Suzanne
marita, amatrix, soror

Canadian Cataloguing in Publication Data

Hall, James Albert, 1934-
    Jungian dream interpretation
(Studies in Jungian psychology by Jungian analysts; 13)
Bibliography: p.
Includes index.
ISBN 0-919123-12-0

1. Dreams. 2. Psychoanalysis. 3. Jung, C.G. (Carl
Gustav), 1875-1961. I. Title. II. Series.

BF1078.H34 1983   154.6'3   C83-098964-1

INNER CITY BOOKS
Box 1271, Station Q, Toronto, Canada M4T 2P4
Telephone (416) 927-0355

Honorary Patron: Marie-Louise von Franz.
Publisher and General Editor: Daryl Sharp.
Editorial Board: Fraser Boa, Daryl Sharp, Marion Woodman.

INNER CITY BOOKS was founded in 1980 to promote the
understanding and practical application of the work of C.G. Jung.

Cover: "Knave and double-headed Queen of Hearts plus many
long matches," 1980. Courtesy Eryl Lauber, Switzerland.

Glossary and Index by Daryl Sharp.

Printed and bound in Canada by Webcom Limited.

CONTENTS

See last page for descriptions of other Inner City Books

Preface

During the first two years of my psychiatric practice I attempted to maintain a neutral attitude toward different theories of dream interpretation. I hoped that by considering all such theories equally valid, I would eventually be able to discriminate on the basis of clinical observation the advantages and disadvantages of each theory. I hoped rationally to decide for myself which theory of dream interpretation seemed preferable.

The two major contenders in this contest of theories were the approaches to dream interpretation of Freud and Jung. During my medical and psychiatric training the theories of Freud had been exclusively emphasized when dreams were mentioned, if they were mentioned at all. During psychiatric residency at Duke University Medical Center my personal analysis was with Dr. Bingham Dai, a Sullivanian, who emphasized the relation of dream material to early family patterns and ego identities based upon those relationships. I still remember that after seventy-five hours of analysis with him I impatiently remarked, "I *know* about my mother complex, we don't have to find *that* in a dream again!" He laughed kindly, knowing (as I later came to appreciate) the difference between *knowing* as a cognitive content and *knowing* in the sense of lived wisdom. When I left Duke to return to Texas, Dr. Dai's last advice to me was: "Don't get too deeply into Jungian theory too quickly." He sensed, it seems, my later deep attraction to the Jungian view.

It finally became impossible for me to deal with dreams comfortably from a non-Jungian perspective. All other theories of dreams seemed to be special cases of the Jungian view, but it was not possible for me to compress the broad vision of Jung into any other available theory. I became a convinced Jungian.

My own personal Jungian analysis was the primary teacher about the meaning of dreams, for which I am continually grateful to my analysts: Rivkah Scharf Kluger, Dieter Baumann, Marie-Louise von Franz and Edward Whitmont. Work with many analysands over a number of years of clinical practice has brought confirming data. In 1977 I published a basic text on dream interpretation, *Clinical Uses of Dreams: Jungian Interpretations and Enactments,* in which I compared Jungian dream theory with other significant theories, pointing out differences and similarities. I also included a modest attempt to relate Jungian dream theory to the laboratory study of sleep and dreaming.

The present volume does not review these various comparisons, but gives straightforward, practical advice on dream interpretation and its use in light of the basic principles of Jungian psychology. I have highlighted recurrent clinical problems, giving examples and discussion of exactly *why* certain interpretations are preferred, and in most instances demonstrating how these interpretations relate to clinical change. Some useful references are indicated, but there is no intention to provide again an exhaustive review of the growing literature on dream interpretation.

One can give general guidelines for dream interpretation, but it is not possible to give airtight rules of procedure. There is no substitute for one's personal analysis and clinical experience under a skilled supervisor, both essential elements of any psychoanalytic training of whatever school or emphasis.

Dreams used here for clinical illustrations are not presented with the full range of amplification that may occur in an actual analytic hour. Nor, in most cases, have I tried to show the rich matrix of personal meaning into which a dream can be fitted during analysis. These omissions are necessary for the sake of brevity and to allow focus on the clinical problem being illustrated.

All dreams are used with the permission of the dreamer, but similar motifs and types of dreams often occur in different persons. Hence none of my analysands should identify any of the dreams as their own, nor should they take the comments about a dream example as referring to any dream of theirs. These dreams are taken out of the rich matrix of clinical Jungian analysis and presented for particular illustrative purposes.

1

Basic Concepts of Jungian Psychology

Jung used certain terms to describe the different parts of the psyche, both conscious and unconscious. These concepts were empirically derived from observation of a great deal of clinical material, including Jung's early work with the word association experiment, which formed the basis for polygraph testing (modern lie detectors) and for the concept of psychological complexes. (Jung was already deeply involved in word association studies when he first read Freud's *Interpretation of Dreams*, published in 1900.)

It is useful to consider basic Jungian concepts in several categories, although one must remember that the divisions are more or less arbitrary and for convenience of description and discussion; in the living psyche, different levels and various structures function as an organized whole. There are two basic topographical divisions: consciousness and the unconscious. The unconscious is further divided into the personal unconscious and the objective psyche. Jung's earlier term for the objective psyche was "collective unconscious," and this is still the term most widely used in discussing Jungian theory. The term objective psyche was introduced to avoid confusion with various collective groups of mankind, since what Jung particularly wanted to emphasize was that the depths of the human psyche are as objectively real as the outer, "real" world of collective conscious experience.

There are thus four levels of the psyche:

1) *personal consciousness,* or ordinary awareness;
2) the *personal unconscious,* that which is unique to an individual psyche but not conscious;
3) the *objective psyche,* or collective unconscious, which has an apparently universal structure in mankind; and
4) the outer world of *collective consciousness,* the cultural world of shared values and forms.

Within these basic topographical divisions there exist general and specialized structures. The general structures are of two types: archetypal images and complexes. The special

9

structures of the personal parts of the psyche, both conscious and unconscious, are four: the *ego,* the *persona,* the *shadow* and the syzygy (paired grouping) of *animus/anima.* Within the objective psyche there are archetypes and archetypal images, whose number cannot be precisely stated, although there is one notable archetype: the *Self,* which may also be referred to as the central archetype of order.

General Structures

Complexes are groupings of related images held together by a common emotional tone. Jung discovered the presence of emotionally-toned complexes by noting regularities in sub-jects' associations to missed or delayed responses in the word association experiment. He found that in each subject these associations tended to cluster about certain themes, such as associations to the mother—a "mother complex." The term complex has long since passed in a loose way into general cultural usage. Complexes are the basic contents of the per-sonal unconscious.

Archetypal images are the basic contents of the objective psyche. Archetypes themselves are not directly observable, but like a magnetic field are discernible by their influence on the visible contents of the mind, the archetypal images and per-sonified or imaged complexes. The archetype in itself is a tendency to structure images of our experience in a particular fashion, but the archetype is not the image itself. In discussing the concept of the archetype, Jung likened it to the crystal formation in a saturated solution: the lattice-structure of a particular crystal follows certain principles (the archetype), while the actual form a particular crystal will take (archetypal image) cannot be predicted in advance. Everyone is born with a tendency to form certain images, but not with the images themselves. There is a universal human tendency, for exam-ple, to form an image of the mother, but each individual forms a particular mother image based on this universal human archetype.

Archetypal images are fundamental and deep images formed by the action of archetypes upon the accumulating experience of the individual psyche. Archetypal images differ from the images of complexes in having a more universal and generalized meaning, often with numinous affective quality. Archetypal images that are meaningful to a large number of persons over an extended period of time tend to be embedded culturally in collective consciousness. Examples in cultural form are the image of the king and queen, the Virgin Mary, and such religious figures as Jesus and Buddha. Many collective figures and situations carry archetypal images without anyone being ordinarily aware of the projection. The strong emotional reactions after the assassination or death of a public figure, such as a president or king, movie star or religious leader, show that for many persons the particular figure carried an archetypal projection.

Any recurrent human experience has an archetypal foundation: birth, death, sexual union, marriage, conflict of opposing forces, etc. Although archetypes may have evolved, they are such a slow variable that for all practical purposes they may be considered as fixed within historical time.

In Jung's model the Self is the regulating center of the entire psyche, while the ego is only the center of personal consciousness. The Self is the ordering center which actually coordinates the psychic field. It is additionally the archetypal template of individual ego-identity. The term Self is further used to refer to the psyche as a whole. There are thus three separable meanings of Self:

1) the psyche as a whole, functioning as a unit;
2) the central archetype of order, when viewed from the point of view of the ego; and
3) the archetypal basis of the ego.

Because the Self is a more comprehensive entity than the ego, the perception by the ego of the Self often takes the form of a symbol of higher value: images of God, the sun as the center of the solar system, the nucleus as the center of the atom, etc. The affective tone of an experience of the Self is often numinous or fascinating and inspiring of awe. The ego experiencing the Self may feel itself to be the object of a superior power. When the ego is unstable the Self may appear as a reassuring symbol of order, often in the form of a mandala, a figure with a clear periphery and a center, such as a quadrated circle or a square within a circle, although the forms are capable of endless elaboration. In Eastern religious traditions, mandala arrangements often contain god-images and are used in meditational practices. Although the Self is the least empirical of Jung's structural concepts—because it is at the borderland of what can be clinically demonstrated—it is a useful term in describing psychologically what is otherwise indescribable. Indeed, phenomenologically the Self is virtually indistinguishable from what has traditionally been called God.

Relation between the Personal and the Objective Psyche

Our point of reference in the psyche is the ego complex, that structure we refer to whenever we use the first-person singular pronoun "I." The personal layers of the psyche, however, rest upon an archetypal foundation in the objective psyche or collective unconscious. The personal sphere, both conscious and unconscious, develops out of the matrix of the objective psyche and is continually related to these deeper areas of the psyche in a profound and organic fashion, although the developed ego inevitably tends naively to consider itself the center of the psyche. It is similar to the difference between the sun revolving around the earth or vice versa.

The activity of the deeper layers of the psyche is clearly experienced in dreaming, a universal human experience, and it may break through in excessive form in acute psychosis. In an intensive Jungian analysis the analysand comes to appreciate the essentially helpful movements of the objective psyche in furthering the empirical individuation process of the ego. Some analysands learn the Jungian technique of active imagination, through which it is possible intentionally to contact these deeper layers of the psyche during waking life.

In structural terms, each complex in the personal sphere (conscious or unconscious) is formed upon an archetypal matrix in the objective psyche. At the core of every complex is an archetype. The ego is formed upon the archetypal core of the Self; behind the personal mother complex is the Great Mother archetype; the imago of the father and mother together has at its center the archetypal image of the divine parents; and there are deep archetypal roots for the shadow and for many persona roles. An archetypal form may involve the combination of separable forms; for example the divine marriage or *hieros gamos* can also image the unification of opposites. The archetypal layer of the psyche has the ability to form symbols that in effect unite contents that are irreconcilable at the personal level. This ability of the objective psyche to form reconciling symbols is called the *transcendent function* because it can transcend the conscious tension of opposites. In this process conflicts do not necessarily disappear, rather they are transcended and relativized.

Because each complex in the personal psyche rests upon an archetypal foundation in the objective psyche, any complex that is penetrated to sufficient depth will reveal its archetypal associations. Much of the art of Jungian analysis lies in amplifying images to the point where the ego experiences its connection to the archetypal world in a healing fashion, but not to such an extent that the ego is swamped in a sea of non-unified archetypal contents. For example, if the ego is able to experience its connection to the Self, an ego-Self axis is formed and the ego thereafter has a more abiding sense of its relation to the very core of the psyche. But if a weak or undeveloped ego has this experience, it may be assimilated by the Self, appearing as psychic inflation and the loss of a clear standpoint in consciousness, or, at worst, temporary psychosis. The frequent experience of "being God" when taking psychedelic drugs such as LSD and psilocybin is an experience by the drugged ego of its archetypal core in the Self, but without sufficient grounding in reality to establish a stable ego-Self axis.

Complex and Archetype

Each complex is a group of related images formed about a central core of meaning that in its essence is archetypal. From the moment of first awareness, these archetypal possibilities of the psyche are filled in with personal experience, so that the adult ego feels that conscious, subjective contents are simply the sum of its own past personal experiences. It is often only in analysis, in dreams, or in very moving emotional experiences that the developed ego can experience the true archetypal foundations of the complexes. In the practice of analysis many imaginal techniques may be used to facilitate this awareness: guided imagination, gestalt techniques, drawing, work in clay, dancing, construction of projective forms in a sandtray, hypnoanalytic techniques, or, the most pure form, active imagination. For individuation to proceed most directly the ego must always take a stance toward the contents of the objective psyche that are revealed in these activities—not simply evoke them, like the sorcerer's apprentice.

Since each complex holds personal images in an archetypal matrix, there is always a danger that the personal associations will be mistaken for the core of the complex, leading to a merely reductive analysis, i.e., interpreting current conflicts purely in the light of early childhood experiences. Conversely, the excessive archetypal amplification of images may lead to some understanding of the archetypes but is likely to miss the healing connection between the personal and the objective psyche.

In order to better understand the dynamic interaction between the various psychological structures conceptualized by Jung, it is helpful to separate them into two categories: identity structures and relational structures. The ego and the shadow are primarily identity structures, while the persona and the anima or animus are primarily relational structures. In the natural process of individuation, there seems to be first a need for the formation of a strong and reliable ego with which to establish oneself in the world. This is followed by the task of relating to other persons and to the collective culture in which one exists. It is usually not until later in life that the ego experiences a need to relate to the archetypal forces that lie behind both the collective culture and the personal psyche —a need that often appears as a so-called mid-life crisis.

Identity Structures: Ego and Shadow

A basic ego-identity is formed quite early, at first embedded in the mother-child dyad, later enlarged within the family unit and still later expanding to include an ever-widening cultural environment. In the process of ego formation, certain innate activities and tendencies of the individual will be accepted by the mother or the family and other activities and impulses will be negatively valued and thus rejected. The crisis of toilet-training stands for many other more subtle interactions in which the ego-identity of the growing child is molded by the preferences and dislikes of those persons it is dependent upon. The tendencies and impulses which are rejected by the family are not simply lost; they tend to cluster as an alter-ego image just below the surface of the personal unconscious. This alter-ego is what Jung termed the *shadow,* because when one part of a pair of opposites is brought into the "light" of consciousness, the other rejected part metaphorically falls into the "shadow" of unconsciousness.

Since the contents or qualities of the shadow were potentially part of the developing ego, they continue to carry a sense of personal identity but of a rejected or unacceptable kind, and usually associated with feelings of guilt. Since the shadow was dynamically disassociated from the dominant ego-identity in the course of early development, its possible return to claim a share of conscious life arouses anxiety. Much of the routine work of psychotherapy and analysis is to create a place in which it is safe to again examine the contents of the shadow and possibly integrate much that was previously discarded by early "splitting" in the formation of the ego. Many natural attributes of the psyche that are disassociated in childhood are actually necessary for healthy adult functioning. Aggressive and sexual impulses, for example, are often dissociated, since their expression in childhood would be inappropriate or culturally unacceptable and troublesome to parents; but these are qualities essential to the normal adult personality, where they can be modulated and integrated in a fashion not available to the immature ego structure of the child. Other qualities, even the easy expression of innate intelligence, may be similarly dissociated into the shadow.

The conscious integration of contents of the shadow has the dual effect of enlarging the sphere of activity of the ego and releasing the energy previously needed to maintain the dissociation and repression of those shadow qualities. The individual often experiences this as a new lease on life.

Because the shadow is potentially ego, it tends to have the same sexual identity as the ego, masculine in a man and feminine in a woman. In addition to being personified in dreams and fantasy material, the shadow is commonly found projected upon persons of the same sex, often someone both disliked and envied for having qualities that are not sufficiently developed in the dominant image of oneself.

Relational Structures: Anima/Animus and Persona

The enhanced ego-identity formed through assimilation of parts of the shadow is faced more clearly with the need to relate to others, both to other persons and to the transpersonal culture of the collective conscious world and the transpersonal archetypal contents of the objective psyche. The two structural forms that facilitate this relational task are the anima or animus and the persona.

Qualities that are culturally defined as inappropriate to the sexual identity of the ego tend to be excluded even from the shadow alter-ego and instead constellate around a contrasexual image: a masculine image (animus) in the psyche of a woman and a feminine image (anima) in the psyche of a man. Jung observed such images in the dreams and fantasy material of his patients, realizing that these images carried such importance that estrangement from them could produce a feeling that primitive cultures would describe as "loss of soul."

The usual way in which the anima or animus is experienced is in projection upon a person of the opposite sex. Unlike the projection of the shadow, such projection of the anima or animus lends a quality of fascination to the person who "carries" them in projected form. "Falling in love" is a classic instance of mutual anima and animus projection between a man and a woman. During such a mutual projection one's sense of personal worth is enhanced in the presence of the person who represents the soul image in projected form, but a corresponding loss of soul and emptiness may result if the connection is not maintained. This projective phase, the unconscious identification of another person with the soul image in one's own psyche, is always limited in time; it inevitably ends, with varying degrees of animosity, because no actual person can live up to the fantastic expectations that accompany a projected soul image. And with the end of projection comes the task of establishing a genuine relationship with the reality of another person.

Considered as structures of the psyche, the soul images of anima and animus, even in projection, have the function of enlarging the personal sphere of consciousness. Their fascination enlivens the ego and pulls it toward ways of being that have not yet been integrated. The withdrawal of the projection, if accompanied by integration of the projected contents, inevitably leads to increased awareness. If the projected anima or animus is not integrated when the projection is withdrawn, the process is likely to occur again with someone else.

The intrapsychic function of the anima or animus, its role within the individual, is directly analogous to the way it works in projected form: leading the individual out of accustomed ways of functioning, challenging one to widen horizons and move toward a more comprehensive understanding of oneself. This intrapsychic function can often be followed in a series of dreams or seen in artistic productions, such as the Victorian novel *She* by Rider Haggard that was frequently cited by Jung. Rima, the bird-woman of the novel *Green Mansions,* is a less complex example. Leonardo's painting of the Mona Lisa captures the mysterious and enigmatic fascination of an anima figure, while Heathcliff in *Wuthering Heights* is a classic portrayal of the animus; Offenbach's great opera *Tales of Hoffmann* deals entirely with the difficulties of integrating various forms of the anima, all with their inevitable fascination.

Because the image of the anima or animus is an unconscious structure, or exists at the very border of the personal unconscious and the objective psyche, it is essentially abstract and lacks the subtle qualities and nuances of an actual person. For this reason, if a man identifies with his anima, or a woman with her animus, the conscious personality loses the capacity for discrimination and the ability to deal with an intricate interplay of opposites.

In traditional European culture (in which Jung lived most of his early life) the anima of a man tended to carry his unintegrated emotional side, and therefore was likely to manifest in a certain sentimentality rather than mature and integrated feeling. Similarly, the animus of the traditional woman was likely to appear as undeveloped thinking and intellect, often in opinionated thoughts rather than logically formulated positions.

It is essential not to confuse these historical and cultural stereotypes with the functional role of the anima and animus as soul figures. With the increasing cultural freedom for both men and women to adopt non-traditional roles, the general content or appearance of the anima and the animus is indeed changing, but their essential role as guide or psychopomp remains as clear as in Jung's first descriptions. The partial integration of the anima or animus (which cannot be as complete as that of the shadow) contributes to an individual's ability to deal with the complexity of other persons as well as the other parts of one's own psyche.

The *persona* is the function of relationship to the outer collective world. Persona is a term derived from the Greek word for "mask," carrying overtones of the comic and tragic masks of classical Greek drama. Any culture provides many recognized social roles: father, mother, husband, wife, physician, priest, advocate, etc. These roles carry with them generally expectable and acceptable ways of functioning in the particular culture, often even including certain styles of dress and behavior. The developing ego chooses various roles, integrating them more or less into the dominant ego-identity. When the persona roles fit well—that is, when they truly reflect the abilities of the ego—they facilitate normal social interaction. The physician wearing the white coat, and psychologically "wearing" the persona of the medical profession, is more easily able to perform necessary (and potentially embarrassing) examinations of the patient's bodily functioning. (The converse persona, that of the patient, is one physicians have notorious difficulty assuming when they themselves are ill.)

The healthy ego can more or less successfully adopt different persona roles according to the appropriate needs of a given situation. The shadow, in contrast, is so personal that it is something one "has" (if indeed it does not have the ego at times). There are persona malfunctions, however, that often require psychotherapeutic intervention. Three are most prominent: 1) excessive development of the persona; 2) inadequate development of the persona; and 3) identification with the persona to such an extent that the ego mistakenly feels itself to be identical with the primary social role. Excessive persona development can produce a personality that precisely fills the social roles, but leaves one with a sense that there is no real person "inside." Insufficient persona development produces a personality that is overly vulnerable to the possibility of rejection and hurt, or of being swept up into the persons with whom it relates. The usual forms of individual or group psychotherapy are of great help in these conditions.

Identification with the persona is a more severe problem in which there is an insufficient sense of the ego being separable from the social persona role, so that anything that threatens the social role is experienced as a direct threat to the integrity of the ego itself. The "empty nest syndrome"—ennui and depression when one's children leave home—betrays an over-identification with the persona of the parental role and can occur in both men and women. The person who feels empty and adrift except when working has misused the persona appropriate to work or profession and has failed to cultivate a wider sense of identity and competency. Analytic treatment is frequently needed to work through severe problems of identification with the persona.

The Individuation Process

Individuation is a central concept in Jungian theory. It refers to the process in which a person in actual life consciously attempts to understand and develop the innate individual potentialities of his or her psyche. Because the archetypal possibilities are so vast, any particular individuation process inevitably must fail to achieve all that is innately possible. The important factor, therefore, is not the amount of achievement, but whether the personality is being true to its own deeper potentialities rather than simply following egocentric and narcissistic tendencies or identifying with collective cultural roles.

The ego may identify with structures in the personal unconscious that are not in harmony with the broader individuation process. This most frequently causes neurosis—a feeling of being split apart, never one in response and feeling. Living a family role assigned in childhood may produce such neurotic splitting, as can an attempt to avoid moving forward through the stages of life, fixating oneself at an earlier level.

The ego may also be out of touch with its individuation process as a result of identifying with roles offered it in the collective spheres—either the roles of the collective unconscious, in which the ego identifies with an archetype and becomes inflated, or those offered in collective consciousness— social roles—becoming something that, however valuable, is not true to the individual fate. Identification with a social role (identification with the persona), even if that role is accepted and well rewarded by a wide segment of a society, is not individuation. Jung felt that Hitler and Mussolini exemplified such identification with figures from the collective unconscious, leading both themselves and whole nations to tragedy.[1]

The extreme of identification with an archetypal role in the objective psyche (collective unconscious) results in a psychotic identification with a figure that is larger (and less human) than the ego. Some archetypal identifications are confusions of the ego with a cultural hero or savior figure—Christ, Napoleon, the mother-of-the-world, etc. Even negative identifications may achieve archetypal proportions (negative inflation), as in persons with a psychotic depression who feel they have committed the "unpardonable sin," placing themselves, by implication, even above God's power to forgive.

It is difficult to describe a successful or typical process of individuation because each person must be considered a unique case of one. Certain "norms" can be stated, such as comparing the usual process of individuation to the course of the sun—rising toward clarity and definition during the first half of life and declining toward death in the second half[2]— but such generalizations have constant exceptions when one deals with individuals at close range, as in the process of analysis.

In his emphasis on the process of individuation as a central concept of analytical psychology, Jung spoke clearly for the deep importance and value of the unique human life. This priority is echoed in the great world religions, but is missing in many modern mass movements, where the individual is reduced to a social, economic or military unit. In this sense, individuation is a counterpoint to the threatened loss of human value in a world that is excessively organized on technological or ideological grounds.

Throughout his life Jung maintained a great interest in religious experience. He involved himself in the study of Eastern religions, understood alchemy as a non-orthodox religious and psychological practice, and explored the transformation rituals he found still active within the Western Christian tradition. Since the Self appears phenomenologically with the same imagery that has often been associated with the deity, it functions to some extent as a God-image within the psyche. The relation between this image and what theological speculation has referred to as God is indeed an open question, although not one that is frequently opened. Numinous experiences occur in some dreams and seem capable, if assimilated, of producing deep and lasting alterations in the personality structure, an effect parallel to some religious conversions and to some peak experiences in waking life.

The individuation process, as understood in Jungian theory and encouraged in analysis, involves a continuing dialogue between the ego, as the responsible center of consciousness, and a mysterious regulating center of the total psyche, a center Jung called the Self—both the core of the ego and transcendent to it, needing the ego for the individuation process to unfold yet seemingly separate and independent of ego states. We do not know the nature of the Self; it is a concept needed to discuss observable activities of the psyche but not capable of direct elucidation.

A "successful" Jungian analysis leads one to appreciate the ultimately mysterious nature of the psyche, which seems both intimate and transpersonal, both bound by the individual ego and yet freer in time and space than the empirical personality. At this borderland of the psyche we are at the door of larger cultural questions that cannot be answered by clinical insight alone.

2

The Nature of Dreaming

Dreaming is a universal human experience. In a phenomenological sense, a dream is an experience of life that is recognized, in retrospect, to have taken place in the mind while asleep, although at the time it was experienced it carried the same sense of verisimilitude that we associate with waking experiences; that is, it seemed to happen in a "real" world that was only in retrospect acknowledged to be a "dream" world.

The phenomenology of dreams involves events that are not experienced in the waking world: sudden shifts of time and place, changes in age, the presence of persons known to be deceased or of fantastic persons and animals that never existed. Perhaps the most radical shift experienced in a dream is the shift of the ego-identity itself from one character to another, or perhaps to no character at all, the dream-ego seeming to observe events as if from an omniscient floating position.

During the last several decades, an immense amount of work has been done on neurophysiological states associated with dreaming. Thus far such studies have allowed investigators to define with some precision when a sleeping subject is in a REM state, a state of ascending Stage 1 sleep with rapid eye movements. When awakened in such a REM state there is a high probability (but no certainty) that the subject will report having been dreaming just prior to awakening. There are some dream reports, however, from non-REM stages of sleep. Although there were early intriguing studies that seemed to link the direction of eye movements to the content of experienced dreams,[3] that observation still lacks sufficient confirmation to be generally accepted.

Since the REM state occupies a majority of the time of premature infants, and decreases steadily during the aging process, it would seem to be a biologically determined state rather than one simply serving the psychological needs of the subject. REM sleep is found also throughout most animal spe-

cies, where psychological factors are not a major consideration. It may initially represent a processing of information
related to binocular vision, or may serve the purpose of peri-
odically alerting the central nervous system during the night.

Whatever the biological basis of dreaming, it seems in the
human to serve some process necessary to healthy psychological functioning. Freud assigned to the dream the role of
guarding sleep from the irruption of repressed impulses, a
position not generally thought to be in accord with more
modern dream research. In contrast, Jung's position was that
the dream compensated the limited views of the waking ego, a
purpose in harmony with the information-processing hypothe-
sis of dreaming, but expanding far beyond mere assimilation
of new data.

Dreams as Compensation

The dream in Jungian psychology is seen as a natural, regula-
tory psychic process, analogous to compensatory mechanisms
of bodily functioning. The conscious awareness by which the
ego guides itself is inevitably only a partial view, for much
remains always outside the sphere of the ego. The unconscious
contains forgotten material as well as material such as the
archetypes that cannot in principle be conscious, although
changes in consciousness can point toward their existence.
Even within the field of consciousness some contents are in
focus while others, although indispensable to the maintenance
of the focal awareness, are not.[4]

There are three ways in which the dream may be seen as
compensatory, and all are important in understanding the
clinical use of dreams. First, the dream may compensate temporary distortions in ego structure, directing one to a more
comprehensive understanding of attitudes and actions. For
example, someone who is angry at a friend but finds the anger
quickly waning may dream of being furious at the friend. The
remembered dream brings back for further attention a quan-
tity of anger that had been suppressed, perhaps for neurotic
reasons. It may also be important for the dreamer to realize
which complex was constellated (activated) in the situation.

A second and more profound mode of compensation is the

way in which the dream as a self-representation of the psyche may face a functioning ego structure with the need for a closer adaptation to the individuation process. This generally occurs when one is deviating from the personally right and true path. The goal of individuation is never simply adjustment to existing conditions; however adequate such adjustment seems, a further task is always waiting (ultimately the task of facing death as an individual event). An example of this second type of compensation is the dream of a person who was quite well adapted socially, in the community, family and work areas of life. He dreamed that an impressive voice said, "You are not leading your true life!" The force of that statement, which awoke the dreamer with a start, lasted for many years and influenced a movement toward horizons that were not clear at the time of the dream.

These two forms of compensation—the dream as a "message" to the ego and as a self-representation of the psyche—comprise the classical Jungian idea of the compensatory function of dreams, substantially different from the traditional Freudian view of dreams as wish-fulfilment or protectors of sleep.

It is becoming increasingly clear to me, however, that there is a more mysterious and more subtle third process by which dreams are compensatory. The archetypal core of the ego is the enduring basis of "I" but can be identified with many personae or ego-identities. The dream may be seen as an attempt to directly alter the structure of complexes upon which the archetypal ego is relying for identity at more conscious levels. For instance, many dreams seem to challenge the dream-ego with various tasks, the achievement of which may alter the structure of the waking-ego, since the identity of the dream-ego is most often a partial identity of the waking-ego. Events are experienced by the dream-ego as interactions with "outer" situations within the structure of the dream; but the outer events of the dream may directly reflect complexes that are involved in the day-to-day functioning and structure of the waking-ego. Changes in the relationship with these dream situations can be experienced by the waking-ego as a change in its own attitude or mood. Marie-Louise von Franz gives a particularly clear example of this type of compensation from one of her own dreams. After a day of feeling the nearness of death she dreamed that a romantic young boy—an animus figure—had died.[5]

In the usual course of Jungian analysis dreams are often used as a point of reference for the interaction of the analytic process. Analyst and analysand are allies in attempting to understand the "message" of the dream in relation to the ego of the analysand. At times dreams indicate that attention should be directed to the transference-countertransference, the particular constellation of interaction in the analytic situation. Since there is no privileged position from which one can know the "truth" of another person's psyche, analyst and analysand are engaged in an exploratory venture that involves basic trust between them. If the dream focuses on that relationship, the relationship must be examined analytically.

In interpreting dreams, it is important never to feel that the dream has been exhausted. At best one can find a useful, current meaning to the dream, but even this may be modified in the light of subsequent dreams, for dream interpretation involves a continuing dialogue between the ego and the unconscious, a dialogue that extends indefinitely and whose subject matter may shift both in focus and in level of reference.

Even when dreams are not interpreted they seem at times to have a profound effect upon waking consciousness. From observation of the impact of unanalyzed dreams, it is possible to infer that even when not remembered dreams are a vital part of the total life of the psyche.[6] In the Jungian view, dreams are continually functioning to compensate and complement (a milder form of compensation) the ego's waking view of reality. The interpretation of a dream permits some conscious attention to be paid to the direction in which the process of individuation· is already moving, albeit unconsciously. When successful, such a teaming of conscious will and unconscious dynamism furthers the process of individuation more rapidly than is possible when dreams are left unexamined.

An additional benefit from the interpretation of dreams is that the ego retains in conscious memory a residue of the dream, allowing the person to identify similar motifs in everyday life and take the appropriate attitude or action, resulting in less need for unconscious compensation of that particular problem area.

Non-Interpretive Uses of Dreams

The personifications in dreams, including images of scenes and inanimate objects, reflect the structure of psychological complexes in the personal unconscious, all of which rest upon archetypal cores in the objective psyche and all of which are subject to the centering and individuating force of the Self or central archetype. Those particular complexes which are objectified and imaged in the dream (including the particular constellation of the dream-ego) reflect the autonomous activity of the Self in relation to the ego (both waking-ego and dream-ego). It is therefore possible to see, if only dimly, what the Self is doing with the complexes that comprise the ego and other contents of the psyche. Such observations may be used in non-interpretative ways, which is in fact their most usual use in non-Jungian therapies.

The motifs of a dream may refer to the present or the past, and may indicate actual persons, living or dead, or figures that are unknown in waking life. Persons that are not known in waking life are more likely to be personified parts of the dreamer's own psyche. By careful attention to these details it is possible to infer what parts of the psyche and what parts of the ego's past experience are constellated in the mind at the time of the dream. Psychotherapeutic attention to those areas, even without formal interpretation of the dream, may lead the therapeutic process in the same direction as the natural flow of individuation.

When complexes are enacted, as in gestalt techniques, additional psychic energy is focused upon them and the outcome is likely to be increased awareness. Such enactment, however, does not constitute the same use of the dream as does Jungian interpretation, for the focus in such enactments is upon the complex that is constellated and not upon the use made of that complex in the total structure of the dream.

When the clinician has acquired skill in the use of dream interpretation, dreams may serve as an added factor in diagnostic and prognostic evaluation, as well as serving as a subtle indicator of when to institute or alter medication, consider hospitalization, and vary the frequency of psychotherapeutic appointments. A very seriously ill young schizophrenic, for example, often dreamed of his car beginning to roll backward out of control just before he developed an exacerbation of his psychotic symptoms and required increased medication. In several instances the reverse seemed true—he would dream of marked successes or mastery (such as easily defeating the mythological Minotaur) when he was beginning a phase of improvement. He once dreamed that a circus con man had all the parts for an atomic bomb except for the piece the dream-ego had. The dream-ego lied about having the part when the con man asked for it. This seemed at the time to represent an averted "explosion" of his psychotic process, paralleling his conscious reparative efforts. (Many years and many therapists later this young man committed suicide; his last dreams are unknown to me.)

Dreams can be taken as referring to the other material discussed in the analytic hour in which they are reported or to the group therapy session in which they are mentioned, and to the specific life situation of the dreamer at the time of the dream. Careful reference of the dream images to the context of the waking-ego at the time of the dream minimizes the most serious error in the clinical use of dreams: the therapist projecting onto the dream his own thoughts about the patient, rather than using the dream as a corrective message from the unconscious of the patient.

Dream Interpretation and Imaginal Techniques

Modern psychotherapy makes use of many imaginal techniques other than dream interpretation. Imaginal techniques are enactments designed to utilize human imagination, often conceptualized as increased activity of the right cerebral hemisphere, to modify inappropriate assumptions and identities that underlie neurotic unhappiness. I have referred to such imaginal techniques as *enactments* to differentiate them from *acting-out,* which is the unconscious (and generally undesirable) structuring of experience according to unrecognized, unconscious conflicts.[7]

Both dream interpretation and imaginal techniques appear to influence the pattern of complexes in the mind, as do emotional experiences in everyday life and in psychotherapy. Working with dreams is perhaps the most direct and natural approach to altering the complexes, while the next most direct is Jung's method of active imagination, in which unconscious contents are encouraged to "come up," while the ego maintains its waking role of mediating the conflicting pressure of constellated opposites in the psyche.

Other imaginal techniques include hypnoanalytic imagery, painting and molding images from the unconscious, the use of sandplay to construct scenes with small figures in a tray of sand, psychodrama, guided imagination and meditational practices in which a free flow of imagery is permitted. The resulting material is so closely akin to that which appears in dreams that an understanding of the clinical use of dreams should be a fundamental discipline for the use of all imaginal techniques in psychotherapy.

Ego-Identity and the Structure of Complexes

In most clinical uses of dreams, the aim is to help the dreamer see clearly the various forms of his or her own personality structure that are usually unconscious and simply acted out in the world, often causing the neurotic unhappiness that motivates a person to seek professional help. This work by the therapist is essentially similar to the natural spontaneous activity of dreams, for dreams are already attempting to lead the person out of his neurosis and into the process of individuation. Dreams are not dreamed to be analyzed and understood, but an understanding of dreams tells us where the unconscious is already trying to alter the ego-image in the direction of health and individuation.

Health and individuation, however, are not always aligned; what is "healthy" for one dominant ego-image at a particular stage of life may be decidedly *un*healthy for the nascent ego-image of the *next* stage of life. Psychologically, as in other areas of life, the good is the enemy of the better. Individuation is a larger and more complex concept than "health." Individuation is a dynamic process; it involves constant change and eventually leads to an acceptance of the finitude of life and the inevitability of death.

Changes in mood may be visualized as changes in the structure of complexes underlying the image of the ego. To some degree, the ego is capable of making such alterations, as when one reminds oneself of important personal priorities in a situation of ambivalence. This may be no more serious than remembering the intention to lose weight when faced with a menu of attractive desserts. In dealing with more important issues, requiring more profound levels of identity change, however, the necessary alterations are not within the sphere of conscious ego choice. At that level the ego must simply do what it can and then wait upon the action of the transcendent function, the symbol-making capacity of the psyche, which is able to alter the conflict of opposites through creation of a symbolic solution that relativizes both warring opposites in a wider frame of meaning.

Clinical work with dreams involves helping the ego do what is within its power to do. While the underlying necessary transformations can at times be observed in dream images, they cannot be ordered up at the will of either the patient or the analyst. The answer to the insistent (and understandable) cry of the patient to be told "what to *do*" is to do what one can, follow as closely as possible the forms in which the conflict presents itself, make whatever impact one can on the situation—and then wait, watch and trust. Support of this process is an important ingredient in the transformation of the psyche. The analytical situation (and the person of the analyst) may be the only *temenos* the patient has, a safe place where life is held together during the unsettling movement from an old ego-image toward an emerging, more comprehensive one.

The crucial point to remember is that the ego-image itself may alter depending upon which complex (or combination of complexes) the ego uses for a dominant identity. This is fairly easy to see in shadow projections, where the ego feels "justified" in actively not liking someone (usually of the same sex as the ego) who embodies qualities that (to everyone other than the person doing the projecting) are present in the ego-image of the patient. If such a shadow projection is indeed an integral part of one's own character structure, dreams often show the dream-ego engaged in that shadow activity or attitude.

If the shadow is not projected but is acted out by the ego, a curious type of dream may occur when the shadow is being integrated or is being dissociated from the dominant ego-image. Non-drinking alcholics, for example, not infrequently dream of drinking soon after they have ceased to drink in their daily lives. The same type of dream can be observed in cigarette smokers who give up tobacco. Such dreams, simple in structure, suggest that the pattern of ego-identity in which the shadow activity was embedded still persists, although the ego no longer identifies with it. (To see these dreams simplistically as wish-fulfilment risks miring the ego in past attitudes and behavior patterns, rather than encouraging its movement away from them.)

More complex dreams illustrate the same principle. A middle-aged man who at one time had wanted to be a minister, but who was long-since successful in an unrelated career, had an excessively active sex life, of a counter-phobic quality. While separated from his wife (with whom he still had sexual relations) he had a standing weekly date with a married girlfriend, and at other free moments went to a local pick-up bar, having casual sexual contact with a variety of other women. During this hectic sexual activity, his dreams showed him going to church and taking communion! His shadow contained what had previously been a positive value—his religious commitment and interest—which had been dissociated, perhaps because of an extreme fundamentalist split between sexuality and religiosity.

This example also serves to emphasize that in itself the shadow is not positive or negative. The shadow is simply an alter-ego image personifying those contents that have not been assigned to the conscious personality. The shadow may appear negative from the point of view of the dominant ego-image because of dissociation and partial repression from the ego, but its actual *contents* may be either positive or negative, depending upon the state of the present ego-image.

A complex structure that is attached to the ego-identity is often bipolar, or even more complicated. A relatively simple bipolar complex has two identity patterns (or complexes) arranged in a particular way. One pole is often assigned to the ego as a pattern of identity, while the coordinated opposite pole is either repressed into the shadow (with occasional manifestations) or is projected onto a person in the environment, usually a close family member, where it determines a nonpersonal pattern of relationship between the ego and the person upon whom the opposite pattern is projected. This is essentially an impersonal relational structure, which both interferes with the individuation of the person who unconsciously makes the projection and inhibits the achievement of a stable personal relationship with the person upon whom the projection falls.

Another example of a bipolar structure is a dominance/submission pattern, where one pole of the relationship is considered dominant, the other submissive. In the impersonal relationship based upon such a pattern, most interactions between the two persons in the relationship will fall into that pattern: one will be submissive, the other dominant. But there are often symptomatic evidences of the reversal of the pattern. For instance, a very successful businessman, who had taken care of everyone around him for decades, retired and found that he had irrational fears of sudden illness in which he would feel helpless and dependent. Discussion revealed that the fear of death was not a major component. What he actually feared was experiencing the opposite (dependent and submissive) identity that he had avoided since an early age by compulsive work and taking care of others.

A similar dynamic underlies the not infrequent situation in which an airline pilot or cabin attendant is afraid to fly *as a passenger*. In the case of the cabin attendant, there is no question of being "in control" of the airplane when working, but the symbolic meaning of control is clearly present. There are even more frequent instances of a person afraid to ride as a passenger in an automobile, although perfectly comfortable when driving. I know of at least one case of the reverse: a very dominant and controlling woman, to the point of arrogance, who cannot bring herself to drive a car and must be chauffeured on even minor errands.

It is possible to visualize crudely the movement of the ego

over various identity patterns by picturing the complexes in the personal unconscious as arranged in an irregular "net," with certain groups of complexes clustering in patterns, although each group is in contact with all the other complexes in the network. If the archetypal core of the ego based upon the Self is visualized as a ray of light, the particular complexes illuminated by the "light" would be the current identity of the ego. The area that is illuminated always leaves part of the net dark. This unilluminated network falls into various non-ego structural patterns—the shadow, the anima, etc. If the ego "light" is moved it changes not only the "contents" of the ego, but also the pattern of relationships associated with these contents. In ordinary consciousness, a person is unaware that the ego "light" is movable, and simply considers that the area illuminated "is" the ego.

This metaphorical image of net and light requires further elaboration, for the net is not a fixed structure. In fact, when the ego "lights" an area, it is then able to make alterations in the net of complexes in that area. Since the complexes are all in an interrelated field, any alteration in one will affect the structure of all the others to a greater or lesser degree. The ego not only passively experiences the "net" but actively participates in creating (or dissolving) the structure of the "illuminated" complexes.

The situation becomes even more mysterious and complicated when one realizes that the ego is not the only force that can influence the structure of complexes. They can also be altered by the activity of the Self, both directly (as in the constellation of a particular dream context) or indirectly through the Self leading the ego to face certain conflicts or growth stages that the ego has tried to avoid. Both the ego and the Self, therefore, influence the structure of the complexes upon which the ego relies for its own sense of identity. It is important also to remember that the ego is based upon the archetype of the Self and so in a sense it is the vicar or agent of the Self in the world of consciousness.

A sense of the changing process of identity structures is quite helpful in clinical uses of dreams. The more theoretical and profound questions that dreams involve do not have to be understood in order to do good clinical work with dream interpretation. These larger matters primarily include 1) epistemological questions about the nature of knowing, 2) religious questions about the nature of the knower in relation to the encompassing mystery of existence, and 3) the intermediate range of implementation structures (archetypal motifs) mirrored in myths, fairytales and folklore. These last-named constitute a rich field for the pure study of archetypal symbolism, but must be used with caution in interpreting any particular clinical situation, for the complexity of an individual person is greater than the complexity of any myth.

3

The Jungian Approach to Dreams

There are three major steps in the Jungian approach to dream interpretation:

1) a clear understanding of the exact details of the dream;
2) the gathering of associations and amplifications in progressive order on one or more of three levels—personal, cultural and archetypal; and
3) the placing of the amplified dream in the context of the dreamer's life situation and process of individuation.

There are, as already pointed out, many non-interpretive uses of dreams—such as gestalt enactments of the various dream motifs—which may lead to an understanding of the complexes symbolized in the dream, but these do not necessarily illuminate the meaning of the dream itself, which must always be viewed against the backdrop of the dreamer's life.

A clear understanding of the exact details of the remembered dream is essential to minimize dangers of reductionism. If an analysand merely reports, "I dreamed of work," one does not know if the dream actually deals with the everyday work situation or perhaps is using everyday events to symbolize more intrapsychic processes. "I dreamed of work" is like saying that the play *Hamlet* deals with "family relations." Without close attention to the internal relationship of dream images (particularly over a series of dreams) the analyst is in danger of projecting his or her own theory into the patient's material. If the analyst believes that interpersonal relationships are of primary importance, it is all too easy to "see" dream figures as relating to persons in the outer world. Similarly, over-emphasis on the transference-countertransference relation (the distortions of the analyst-patient relationship based on unconscious dynamics in both) can lead to too many dreams being interpreted in terms of the analytic situation. A form of reductionism to which Jungians are especially liable is what may be called *archetypal reductionism.* Since all complexes are constructed upon an archetypal core, it is *always* possible to overamplify a dream motif toward an archetypal

34

meaning, with the attendant danger of substituting the (often fascinating) archetypal amplifications for the tensions of the individuation process in the dreamer's own life.

Questions needed to fully elucidate a dream are similar to those that would be used to clarify any situation in ordinary discourse or in a well-taken medical history. If a patient tells a doctor of a pain, for example, there are many additional details to be clarified: Is the pain constant or intermittent? If intermittent, what is the frequency of recurrence? Is it a sharp pain or a dull pain? Does it occur in one or several places? If in several, does it seem to start in one place and radiate to others? What increases the pain? What makes it better? Does it awaken the patient from sleep? and so on.

Suppose the analysand reports the image of a turtle in a dream. What is the size of the turtle? Its color? Is it still and dormant or active? Are there any unusual features? I myself have had dreams of turtles fifty meters in diameter or as small as several inches. But the small turtle was able to reach three feet into the air and swallow a large chunk of roast beef in one gulp! A turtle is *not* just a turtle!

Amplification of Images

Amplification of a dream image is analogous to "peeling" the three layers of a complex. First one finds the personal associations—where the image appeared in the patient's life, what he thinks of the image, feels about it, etc. These associations reveal the nature of the complex as it has developed around the archetypal core. A person known to the dreamer may appear in a dream, for example, raising the question as to whether the dream image should be taken *objectively* (referring to the actual person in the outer world) or *subjectively* (using the other person to personify a part of the dreamer's own psyche). In practice, known persons, places or events are quite likely to carry an objective meaning, but they may also refer to intrapsychic realities of the dreamer, especially when accompanied by a strong emotional tone. While it is wise always to keep both possibilities in mind, in clinical dream work from a Jungian point of view the emphasis is usually on the intrapsychic significance of the dream images.

The "middle layer" of a complex contains images that are more cultural or transpersonal, such as the convention of red traffic lights meaning *stop;* white as a bridal color; the President representing the ruling center of the United States, etc. Cultural amplifications are often known to the dreamer consciously, but may not be spontaneously mentioned. If the dreamer indicates assent when a possible cultural amplification is offered by the analyst, it may safely be considered a potential part of the complex behind the dream image.

The third, archetypal level of amplification is a characteristically Jungian addition to the general field of dream interpretation. Archetypes in themselves are not visible, being simply tendencies to structure experience in certain ways. Any image structured by an archetype becomes an image of that archetype (though always conveying less than the total potentiality of the archetype). Archetypal images in dreams are often not recognized, because 1) the analyst may be unaware of the mythological or archetypal significance of a certain motif, and 2) since any recurrent human experience can be archetypal, many archetypal elements are too commonplace to attract attention. Archetypal images are those that have proved meaningful enough to a large number of people over a protracted period of time so as to become an accepted part of some large symbolic system—often depicted in a folktale, fairytale, mythologem or religious system, living or archaic. The psyches of many persons, therefore, have "filtered" an archetypal image.

It is not necessary, in my opinion, to interpret at the archetypal level in order to do generally good dream interpretation in a clinical setting. There are often instances, however, in which an archetypal interpretation is much more meaningful than one on a more personal level. The realization of archetypal images unknown to the conscious mind of the dreamer can open an important theoretical window into the deeper nature of the psyche, and also provide a healthy perspective on our personal everyday dramas.

Context of the Dream

The dream must be read against the context of the dreamer's current life. Jung felt that dreams were most often compensatory to the conscious view of the ego, offering a counterpoint (often a more inclusive viewpoint) to the attitude of the dominant ego-identity. The ego always has a limited view of reality, while the dream manifests a tendency toward enlargement of the ego (although eventual enlargement may temporarily require a more constricted or focused awareness). Placing the dream in the context of the dreamer's life does not support any easy reading of the dream as a clue to future action. Likewise, taking a dream as confirmation of one's present conscious position is too easy in most cases to yield the compensating information that dreams contain. As a general rule, if you already know what the dream seems to be saying, then you have missed its meaning.

When dream interpretation is a routine part of psychotherapy, a context also develops in a series of dreams, so that one can relate an image in a current dream to a similar image in past dreams. The related but different images may be considered different views of the same complex, often giving additional clues as to the underlying meaning.

There are other maxims of dream interpretation, but the three basic movements described above constitute the essence. Our later examination of specific dream examples, as well as the therapist's own experience, will add to an understanding of how these principles are applied in actual practice. Some dreams fit easily into a classic dramatic structure—a situation, complication, climax and result. In such dreams it is often possible to trace unexpected connections between one scene and another, so that what follows is in some sense "caused" by the action of the dream-ego in the preceding scene. It is particularly important to observe the activity (or lack of it) of the dream-ego, often suggesting immediate parallels in waking life. In general, dream activity that takes place without the participation of the dream-ego (or with the dream-ego as an outside, passive observer) tends to be also "outside"—that is, unconscious—in the waking life of the dreamer. Other maxims will be discussed in the following chapters.

4

Dreams as Diagnostic Tools

Initial Dreams in Analysis

In the initial meeting with a prospective analysand, dreams can offer information both as to diagnosis and prognosis. While dream interpretation can never substitute for a thorough clinical interview and mental status examination, dreams can be a great help if properly integrated with the other clinical material.

Inquiry about recent or significant dreams fits naturally into an initial interview, when one is asking questions that allow observations of the patient's intellectual functioning: flow of thought; ability to abstract; orientation as to time, place and situation; recent and remote memory; judgment in real and hypothetical situations; level, congruence and type of affective response; and such optional but interesting aspects of mental functioning as revealed by proverb interpretation. New patients are frequently pleased to be asked about dreams, since in the popular mind dream interpretation is considered a natural part of psychoanalytic practice (*psychoanalysis* in a generic sense, not simply Freudian psychoanalysis). In fact, the public is generally very interested in the meaning of dreams, and even many depth psychologists are ill-prepared to respond to this interest.

Recent dreams, particularly those dreamed after the initial appointment was made but before it actually occurred, may reveal aspects of the patient's current unconscious functioning. Dreams that occur early in analysis sometimes point to the long-range outcome of the presenting problem. A man with a long-standing practice of "cross-dressing," for example, had a dream early in analysis that he was dressed in women's clothes, walking across the parking garage of a hotel, when the clothing began to slip off without his being alarmed. This foreshadowed a successful treatment of the transvestism (which had no elements of homosexuality) within a comparatively short period of therapy (although of course there were crisis periods and difficulties during the treatment).

Another man with problems of sexual identity had two early dreams indicating an eventual resolution of his anxiety. He functioned both homosexually and bisexually, but preferred to be exclusively heterosexual. His homosexual functioning, as well as his anxiety and poor self-esteem, seemed clearly related to oedipal problems; in more psychodynamic terms, he was looking for a male relationship to compensate for what he felt to be an emotionally absent father. His two early dreams showed that the unconscious was prepared to see the problem through to a successful conclusion:

Dream 1:
I was in a "sex den" or cave, sleezy, unpleasant. I finish someone's drink in a ritualistic manner. The scene changes and I am in a tall tree with lots of branches. I can't get down. There are other people around and a radio is playing. I finally realize that no one will get me down and that I must jump. I called out for help, though, and two men came and put a plank from a bridge to the limb where I was hanging.

Dream 2 (two nights later):
I was with a man in a building in Hololulu. We went into the basement to an oriental bath and were flopping around in different pools. Then we sat in chairs with belts on them, like a ride at Disneyworld. He knew how to put the belt on but I had not read the instructions. Nevertheless, I made it to the end of the ride. The chairs went in and out of the water during the ride.

In both of these early dreams, one can see the motif of getting safely down to the ground (Dream 1) or to the end of the ride (Dream 2) without serious accident, but with some tension and anxiety. In the first dream, help materializes only when the dream-ego has accepted responsibility and decides to jump down if necessary. In the second, the dreamer is not as accomplished as his friend, but is able to finish the ride safely anyway. Both these dreams suggested a "good" outcome, in terms of consolidating his masculine identity. Within a few weeks he had begun a satisfying affair with a woman and his homosexual contacts and thoughts diminished; he simultaneously began to feel able to express a more independent position in relation to his parents.

These two dreams are presented here only for their prognostic implications, although there are clearly many other useful views of them as well. Being "up a tree," for instance, colloquially suggests a difficult situation, echoing shamanistic initiation rituals, which were sometimes pictured as taking place in a tree, and on an archetypal level pointing to the theme of the world tree or *axis mundi* – a frequent symbol of the centering process in the individual psyche.

Related Images in a Dream Series

Progress in the dissolution of a neurotic pattern can often be followed in dreams extending over a treatment period of months or even years. A woman with marked disturbances in early family life showed such changes. As a child she had been a principal source of emotional support for an alcoholic father. If she did not try to take care of him, she felt guilty. Her mother was an accomplished professional woman who held out "high" standards of attainment for the girl, but gave her little actual emotional approval. When she went for psychotherapy for problems in her marriage, she decided on divorce, but then fell into a sexual relationship with her former therapist and later married him, only to experience a recurrence of the sexual unresponsiveness she had felt in her first marriage. Attempts at intercourse often left her furious. She then entered Jungian treatment. In both group psychotherapy and individual analysis she was helpful and intellectually insightful, although persistent psychosomatic problems (always related to emotional factors) necessitated several hospitalizations.

A very revealing incident happened in an early group therapy session: she was being her usual helpful and insightful self (similar to her relation with her father), but when a male group member refused her help she burst into a sudden rage, showing for the first time her underlying anger (related to her depression). At about this time she dreamed:

> A mother dog with two grown pups hanging on her teats is dragging herself down the street. One of the pups falls off and is hit by a car. It explodes like a bomb.

This striking image of an exploding puppy became a symbol for her dependency problem and the unconscious anger associated with it. Many situations in waking life could be related to her unconscious identification with either the person who was worn out with taking care of others (the self-sacrificing mother) or the explosive anger that developed from her own dependency (the explosive puppy)—both because the dependency needs were never fully satisfied and because they prevented her from achieving her own adult maturity and independence.

After her second divorce, she continued in analysis but for some time avoided any personal relationship with men. During this period, she dreamed:

> I was in an Egyptian room like in a pyramid. On a raised area, an altar or a bier, an Egyptian princess is in labor and is about to give birth to a child. At the base of the raised area, I was being raped by [a father figure] who held me in one position whenever I tried to escape. I hope that the woman will give birth, so that the woman's husband will come and see the rape and rescue me.

It was clear from this dream that the father complex was much more active in her psychology than was her conflicted relationship with her mother. It also showed the possibility of new life (the incipient birth), suggesting a change not initiated by the ego, but which could possibly lead to the rescue of the dreamer from the unconscious pattern symbolized in the dream as incest with the father.

Significantly, soon after this dream the woman fell into a sexual relationship with the man whose wife had appeared in the dream as the Egyptian princess—a rather obvious projection of the dreamer's internal rescuer onto an actual man. After a brief period of happiness, their relationship ended and she became severely depressed, which she knew was not related entirely to the external triangular situation. After some time, she dreamed:

> I was giving my mother a present and she reacted as she always did in reality—she never liked anything I gave her. I could *never* please her. Then I realized *why* she wasn't pleased —she was dead! There was a doctor there from a soap opera I used to watch when I was in my first marriage and my kids were little. He was a good and helpful doctor in the story.

Although this dream seemed to indicate a new awareness associated with the "death" of the mother complex, there was little immediate change in her clinical depression. She struggled with the idea of moving to another city to get away from the man who still troubled her thoughts. At this time she dreamed what proved to indicate a turning point in her neurosis. She had been greatly depressed the day before the dream and also suffered from her psychosomatic problems. The morning after the dream, she described herself as "hypomanic" and happy and (most importantly) without the psychosomatic discomfort that usually plagued her. Here is the dream:

> I am in a room with my mother [who was dead in the previous dream and also in fact]. I am begging some man to have intercourse with me. He doesn't much want to but agrees because, as he says, "It's the last time." The scene changes and I see a pool of blood with something in it that is either a dead baby or a dead dog. It's a gruesome sight, but somehow it is all right because it would have died anyway.

Her asking the man for sex showed the previously unrecognized *desire* behind what had only been experienced as rape. Her association to the "baby or dog" was to the earlier dream of the exploding puppy. The sense that the father complex underlying her neurotic problems was dissolving was reflected in the words of the man in the dream: "It's the last time." The abrupt disappearance of her difficult psychosomatic symptoms reinforced the interpretation of the dream as indicating a real change in the pattern of complexes, the object-relation pattern that seemed to be the schema of her two basic neurotic identities as either the caretaker or (as here) the one who felt dependent on others. The presence of her mother suggests the involvement of the mother complex as well, but that problem is not the active focus of the dream, nor was it the focus in the dream of the Egyptian princess. There is a sense that the death of the "baby or the dog" is connected with "the last time," as it would be if it were a dog, associated with the explosive puppy representing her dependency problem.

The uncertainty as to whether it was a baby (which might indicate the death of real human possibilities) or a dog (suggesting the sacrifice of an animal instinct that might later reappear in human form) was apparently settled by a dream that occurred the next night:

> I dreamed all night of two things, as if they came in and out of my awareness throughout the night. One was a dead and flattened "cockroach" that had legs all around it. [A drawing of what she had seen resembled a child's drawing of the sun disc with radial beams.] Next to the "cockroach" was a dead mouse that had been carefully wrapped in a little blanket. The mouse had big, blue penetrating eyes, almost like a person.

Her association to the cockroach was to one of the most disgusting things in the world: "a huge Houston cockroach." She noted that the drawing had "excess legs." The form of the cockroach also reminded her of a "yarn-dog" that was popular when she was a teenager (when much of the tense interaction with her father occurred). She remembered having a yarn-dog on her bed, with the yarn "hair" spread radially like the legs of the cockroach. These associations together with the other images in the dream suggested that it was a dead dog in the previous dream rather than a baby. The reasoning is this: if her psyche is concerned with the same constellated complexes in both dreams, what was shown as dead in one dream may be shown as dead in another, although the change in imagery may express a nuance of the complex represented by the different images; since the "dead" things in the second dream are clearly non-human (although the mouse has human-like eyes) it is likely that the preceding dream showed the death of a dog rather than the death of a human potential that would more likely have been symbolized by a dead baby.

This series of dreams illustrates a number of important points in clinical dream interpretation. First, the sequence of related dream images permits both a sense of prognostic improvement and some understanding of images that might otherwise be more ambiguous. Second, the images over a series of dreams are similar but not identical—the "dog," the "baby or a dog," the flattened "cockroach" and the "dead mouse"— showing that different images can represent the same underlying complex. (Actually, the dead mouse with the human-like eyes could be associated also to an earlier dream in which the dream-ego cooked "a large fish with human eyes," which seemed to have eucharistic connotations, implying self-sacrifice in the service of others.)

Third, the change in the nature or tenor of the dreams coincides with increased activity on the part of the dream-ego. Although not invariable (nor is any "rule" of dream interpretation), it seems that resolution of constellated dream structures often follows an action of the dream-ego, even if the "action" in the dream is simply a change in attitude rather than physical activity. Fourth, this series of dreams illustrates how the dream-ego may become progressively more involved in the neurotic complex structure pictured in the dreams: in the exploding puppy dream the dream-ego is merely a passive observer; in the Egyptian princess dream, the dream-ego wishes to act but cannot; in the dream of begging a man to have intercourse with her, the dream-ego is finally active. Could it be this activity that "causes" the man to announce "it's the last time," and "causes" the death of the cockroach and the mouse? (This is simply to raise the question of cause and effect in dreams, for which there are as yet no definitive answers.)

This woman's extended series of dreams (from which those presented here are intuitively selected) can best be viewed as representing an enduring structure of complexes of a sexualized dominance-submission form. The dream-ego (and the waking-ego) at various times identified with one pole or the other of the pattern. As she moved toward basic clinical improvement, the series ended not in another oscillation between the poles of that pattern but in the "death" of the pattern itself, which pointed psychologically to the depotentiation of the underlying complex.

Differential Diagnosis

Initial dreams may help in differentiating various diagnoses, such as anxiety neurosis or depressive neurosis. Dreams may also be useful in making distinctions between neurosis, psychosis and characterological or organic problems, all of which may present with overlapping symptomatology. Diagnostic terms may be stated differently in various diagnostic systems (such as the *Diagnostic and Statistical Manual II or III* of the American Psychiatric Association), but the basic clinical syndromes remain relatively constant. The basic neurotic patterns present as mixtures of anxiety and depression with various degrees of dissociation.

Depression

Although there are many theories of depression, ranging from purely psychogenic to organic, it is generally true that psychogenic depression is somehow related to anger that is not given sufficient expression in consciousness. Anger typically arises toward some person in the environment, either present or past, and is secondarily turned upon the ego-image itself, resulting in depression. This classic psychological dynamic can often be seen with unusual clarity in dreams, and can serve as a diagnostic indicator.

What would be experienced by the waking-ego as depression is likely to be shown in the dream as aggression toward the dream-ego by another figure. In the case of the woman whose dreams were discussed in the previous section, the depression began to lift when she was the sexual aggressor in the dream of the dead "dog or baby," but in the Egyptian princess dream (when she was still depressed) she was held tightly in an unwanted sexual embrace by an aggressive father-like figure.

Another woman who experienced consciously a mixture of anger and depression, evoked by her husband's involvement with another woman, had dreams of being threatened by various insects and reptiles, but as she took a more assertive stand toward the outer situation her depression began to lift. The change could be followed through changes in the dreams. In an early dream she was alone in the desert at night, surrounded by cactus and scorpions, afraid to move; in a dream a few weeks later, she was walking on a sidewalk on a college campus (something to learn?) where there were many poisonous snakes around but not actually on the sidewalks, and other people were there and it was daytime instead of night. The aggressive, non-human elements in the earlier dreams can be seen as her own unexpressed aggression, indicating the need to assert her true feelings. As she did so, her dream images became less threatening.

Anxiety

A number of classic anxiety dreams can be seen in many patients. There are three major types that deserve notice: 1) dreams of being unprepared for an examination; 2) dreams of being pursued by some threatening person or creature; and 3) dreams suggesting physical danger to the dream-ego, such as dreams of falling or being threatened by natural events—earthquakes, tidal waves, forest fires, etc.—where there is no malicious motive toward the dream-ego. Anxiety may of course take many other forms in dreams, but these three patterns are particularly recurrent.

Examination dreams have a typical form. The dream-ego realizes that an examination is scheduled, usually a final exam for a college or high school course, and for some reason the dreamer is unprepared, having forgotten to study for the exam or to go to the course, or not knowing where the examination is to be held. The dream-ego may also be late for the examination. Such dreams are more structured (and more frequent in my experience) than the more primitive dreams of pursuit and falling. Because examinations represent evaluation by collective standards, they point to persona-anxiety—anxiety about how one appears in the eyes of others, or a fear of not measuring up to a social role: "Is he a good musician?" "Can he really perform his job well?" etc.

Pursuit dreams indicate anxiety of a more primitive nature, but they are not quite so unstructured as dreams of falling or dreams of natural catastrophy, such as earthquakes or the end of the world. It is important to note *what* is pursuing the dream-ego. Is it a person (male or female)? Is it an animal, a monster or "spacemen?" Is the dream-ego pursued by one "thing" or a collective, such as a mob?

At times there are very revealing changes in the person or thing that pursues. At first it may appear frightening, but as it approaches there may be no indication of aggression to justify the fear felt by the dream-ego. One man dreamed there was a large monster in the darkness, coming toward the dream-ego who stood in a pool of light by a streetlamp. But when the "monster" actually reached the light, it was nothing but a mouse. Perhaps in the dark it *was* a monster, but was modified as it approached the "light" of consciousness surrounding the dream-ego. Complexes in connection with the ego (dream or waking) do not behave in the same manner as complexes unattached to the ego and therefore unconscious.

A woman dreamed that when she opened the faucet in her bathroom an angry alligator came out. It pursued her throughout the house, but when she was able to open the front door and guide it out with a broom, it transformed into a friendly puppy in the sunlight (consciousness). Another woman dreamed that she opened the window shade and found a large spider entirely covering the screen of the window, striking terror into the dream-ego. The spider slowly moved, however, and walked down into the front yard (another symbol of consciousness), where it, too, changed into a puppy that was friendly and playful.

The transformation of frightening dream images is similar to what commonly occurs in fairytales: the frog becomes a prince, the beast a handsome young man, etc. Such transformations, particularly those where an animal or thing changes into a person, seem to picture the "desire" of unconscious contents to become conscious and participate in the life of the ego; this appears in dreams as a transformation of their primitive nature and a movement toward the human realm.

The terrifying unknown "thing" that pursues the dream-ego may be threatening to the dream-ego but not threatening to the individuation process in which the ego is embedded. Examine the dream to see if there is any overt indication that the pursuing "thing" is actually trying to harm the dream-ego. It may simply represent an unconscious aspect of the dreamer that is trying to make contact with the ego, although it may become more aggressive and frightening if the dream-ego resists the contact. Remember that the contents or qualities of the shadow almost always appear to the dominant ego-image as severe threats, even though potentially valuable to the ego for the next stage of individuation.

For example, a woman who had worked for many years with a severe negative mother complex dreamed:

I was asleep in my bed, but it seemed to be an older house, one built in the 1920's or 1930's. I heard a loud knocking at the front door and was terrified, because my husband was out of town and I was alone with the children. I realized that I would have to get up to see who it was. I saw a flashlight on the back porch and was very frightened. I pushed the "panic button" of the alarm system, and the alarm went off—but the line was dead. Had it been cut? Again the loud knocking occurred and I knew that I had to see who was at the door. I was afraid, but when I went to the front door it was the police. They had come to tell me that there had been an airplane crash, the flight my husband was on. It was possible that there had been no survivors. I realized how much I loved him and how frightened I was for his safety.

The thing trying to get into her "house" was frightening, and she felt it was trying to hurt her. Instead, when it was actually confronted in the dream, it brought to mind a compensatory feeling of love and concern for her husband—an indication that she had been somewhat unconscious of the depth of her feelings for him. She awoke realizing that he was asleep in the bed beside her, but the effect of the dream was so profound that she hesitated for some minutes to touch him, for fear that he might *not* be there. For hours she felt the impact of the dream, and its lingering meaning caused a profound shift in her awareness of her true love for her husband, whom she had tended to take for granted in the midst of her neurotic concerns.

Physical danger to the dream-ego is not dangerous, of course, to the waking-ego, except where the emotion associated with such a dream might place strain upon the cardiovascular system during sleep. The most widespread type of anxiety dream associated with real physical danger to the dream-ego is the dream of falling. There seems to be no basis for the folk belief that if one "hits the bottom" in such a dream, there will be actual physical death. Rarely, a person does dream of completing the fall by hitting the ground, but if the dream goes on there is usually some shift in the situation or the state of the dream-ego; it may find itself uninjured, or see that the fall was only a few feet, or it may be "dead" in the dream but observing the body, etc.

The most common ending to such dreams is for the dream-ego to "surface" into the waking ego-identity during the fall. This shift of the dream-ego to the waking-ego is a frequent lysis or outcome of dreams and should be noted when it occurs. Such awakenings, apparently premature in terms of the action of the dream, may be seen as an escape from anxiety, but at times they also carry a symbolic meaning: "Wake up to this!" This sense of "waking up" would seem to be part of the purpose of the dream in which the woman was told by the police that her husband might be dead and awakened to an increased awareness of her positive feelings for him.

It is important to look beyond the mere presence of physical danger to the dream-ego and make some assessment of its meaning within the dream, which will vary depending upon the context. A man dreamed that a spear was thrown at him, just missing him, and that he handed the spear back to the "Mongolian horseman" who had thrown it; his motive was to appease the attacker, but his act only inflamed the attacker's anger. This dream points to a not-infrequent motif: the dream-ego is stimulated to be active in its own behalf. The "attacking" figure could be seen as wanting a more aggressive response from the dream-ego. The same motif is suggested by a dream in which a trident is thrown at the dream-ego by a sinister and angry female figure; the dream-ego realizes, however, that the sinister woman has thereby given him a weapon to oppose her with, which he does, freeing a number of "dead" animals that return to life.

Aggression against the dream-ego may thus be in the service of a deeper purpose—the individuation process—which is concerned with the entire pattern of personal development over the whole lifespan, and relates to any particular dominant ego-image at any particular stage of life in the light of this underlying, ongoing process. Because of the individuation process, to which dreams seem deeply connected, action in a dream may seem to oppose the dream-ego while its true purpose is to enlarge or transform the ego in relation to the Self.

Dreams of severe natural disasters such as earthquakes show a background shift of the ego state rather than a force directed against the dream-ego itself. It is theoretically possible that such dreams, on an objective level, could represent an imminent change in the collective situation, as Jung found dreams that seemed to foreshadow the first World War. This is unlikely, however, as Jung himself pointed out in his BBC interview with John Freeman, because today everyone is quite consciously aware of the possibility of world calamities, natural or man-made; such images clearly do not compensate a conscious collective expectation of peace and progress.[8]

Disaster dreams point rather to a potentially abrupt and possibly violent change in the tacit background of the ego-image that has dominated consciousness. They indicate the potentiality of a major shift in ego-image structure. Such changes, if therapeutically contained, can be transformative; if they happen without containment they may presage a severe clinical course of depression, anxiety or even psychosis.

Psychosis

When considering a possible diagnosis of schizophrenia or some other psychotic process, dreams can be of value in both diagnosis and in following the course of the illness. At times dreams can be of some aid in determining when it is advisable to increase medication or perhaps consider other means of increased support for the embattled ego, such as hospitalization. The skill of reading dreams in such a manner is not easy to convey, because there does not seem to be any clear indicator that is invariably present. Such clues as exist are often contextual to the particular dreamer, meaningful in the series of that person's dreams but not easily generalizable to others. The indicator is often, for example, not the dream motif of danger to the individual dream-ego but simply the appearance in the dream of what might be called a bizarre image. An animal walking about without skin, for instance, or an insane person threatening to blow up the world may show a potential worsening of the clinical condition. Such images must always be balanced, however, against the strength of the ego. Psychosis occurs when the pressure of the unconscious processes overwhelms the ego; this may happen by a surge in unconscious pressure or by a decrease in the usual strength of the ego due to excessive stresses or physical factors such as the effect of psychedelic drugs.

There would seem to be need for research in the use of dream images to assess ego stability and psychotic pressure; such studies would require careful comparisons in a well-defined population over an extended period of observation. Such a study would not be easy or inexpensive, but could add to our clinical understanding of the psychological impact of antipsychotic medication. It might also provide some answers to the crucial questions of mind/brain interaction in relation to personality stability.

Physical Problems

It is by no means an easy matter to make organic diagnoses from dream material, although there are many striking examples of such predictions: the dream of an inner "explosion" preceding the leaking of an aortic aneuryism, the appearance of dream figures with gall bladder disease prior to that illness being suspected in the dreamer, etc. In retrospect it is easy to see that dreams may have been indicating an organic problem, but prognostically it is difficult because of the multiplicity of factors to be considered. Dreams normally seem to be compensating the conscious position of the waking-ego. This they do in the service of the individuation process, whose purposes and concerns are not necessarily the same as those of the waking-ego, since individuation serves the potential wholeness of the personality rather than the perfection of any particular ego configuration. Physical illness may be an overwhelming concern of the conscious ego, but it does not seem to be of equal concern to the Self, the originator of dreams.

Dreams appear to make a distinction between the personality and the body, the dream-ego seeming to be associated with the personality rather than with the body. When indicators of actual physical conditions are represented in a dream, they do not usually appear as an illness of the ego-image within the dream; rather, they are likely to be shown in figures other than the dream-ego, perhaps an image that represents the organic body—an animal, the personal mother (the origin of the physical body) or other representations of organic life.

Dreams of Death

Closely related to the question of representation of organic illness is the motif of death in a dream. To dream that one may die, or even that one is dead, is not particularly rare. Patients may remember such dreams with anxiety, fearing that the dream is an indicator of approaching death. But dreams of death are essentially dreams of transformation of the ego-image. As long as the conscious ego identifies with a particular ego-image, anything that threatens the endurance of that particular ego-image will seem to threaten physical death, for the ego is also tightly identified with the body-image—although the frequent dream motif of looking *at* oneself clearly demonstrates the dissociability of the dream-ego from the image of the body.

Death in a dream is quite different from the meaning of death in the ordinary waking context. Dream images are representations of complexes or archetypes. Any number of images may be associated with the same complex or archetype. Such images do not "die." One image transforms into another, a transformation which can often be followed in a series of dreams. The dream sequence examined earlier—involving the "exploding puppy," the "dog or baby," and the "mouse with human eyes"—illustrates the gradual transformation of a dream image over time.

Persons actually approaching organic death have dreams that are not surprisingly different from other dreams anticipating some significant change, like dreams of a journey or dreams of marriage. Such dreams may encourage the waking-ego to focus on conscious concerns and responsibilities rather than on the approaching death of the physical body. There is insufficient observation and research concerning dreams of the dying for any definitive statement to be made. It would seem, however, that dreams are much less concerned with the death of the body than with the individuation process, hence they consider the approaching end of life as they would other major changes within life. Does this suggest that the individual personality survives physical death? Does it mean that physical death is of little more concern to the Self than significant changes of the ego within the lifespan? These are serious questions for science in general and in particular for parapsy-chology and depth psychology.

Principles to Remember

1. The same complexes can be personified by a number of different images.
2. By following a series of dreams and looking for a related but changing structure within them, it is possible to intuitively note:
    a) changing nuances of a complex in relation to other complexes in the same identity pattern, and
    b) prognostic improvement (or worsening) of the identity pattern, such as one of a dominance-submission nature.
3. Dreams early in analysis may indicate both a diagnostic and prognostic element to be considered in the initial clinical evaluation.

5

Questions of Technique

There is one basic truth about technique: the right technique in the hands of the wrong person won't work, while the wrong technique in the hands of the right person *will* work. The successful use of dream analysis in psychotherapy is not simply a question of technical expertise. *No* technique is entirely adequate, for the personal equation of analyst/analysand is more important. It is within that relationship that all dream work or other therapy must take place. The therapeutic relationship is the *temenos* (sacred boundary, the alchemical *vas* or *krater*) in which the transformative process occurs.

Transference and Countertransference

Analysis is a process that cannot be entirely rational, hence it is similar in some respects to other skillful performances, such as the production of music, art or poetry. The rules that govern such productions are not entirely specific, but serve as maxims or general reminders of the guidelines to be observed.

Perhaps the chief responsibility of the analyst or therapist is to maintain what may be called a *transformative field* in which the transformation of the psyche is more likely to occur. Surprisingly, the transformation may occur in either the analysand (the usual intent) or the analyst—or in both! It is impossible to construct an interpersonal situation in which influences flow in only one direction. Freud's early view was that the analyst could be entirely objective, serving as a virtual "blank screen" onto which the analysand projected his own psychology and relived his neurotic process within the curative boundary of the psychoanalysis. It soon became apparent, however, that in addition to the transference distortions of the analyst by the patient, there were also distortions of the patient by the analyst—the so-called countertransference.

Jung's own views on the subject take this "field" quality clearly into account. In "The Psychology of the Transference," Jung shows that the analyst and analysand are jointly involved in a process that cannot be entirely conscious and may be

54

transformative of both partners.[9] He sees transference and countertransference, moreover, as specific forms of projection, which automatically happens in any relationship.

The analytic situation, nevertheless, is designed to maximize the transformative field for the patient, while minimizing disruptive countertransference by the analyst. The patient's material is discussed in great depth, both historically and in the light of current dreams, while the analyst makes relatively few personal remarks, even though it is impossible for the analyst to be the classic blank screen. In addition, the trained analyst has been through a lengthy period of personal analysis and is presumably more aware of the possibility of projecting his or her own complexes onto the analysand.

How do dreams enter into the transformative field of the analytic relationship? In most instances, the analysand dreams, brings the dream to the analyst, and together they look for the meaning of the dream in the life of the patient. The analyst and analysand are thus colleagues in exploring the unconscious material of the analysand and relating it to his or her ongoing process of individuation. There are times, however, when working with dreams may place stress on this usual pattern. This regularly happens in the following instances:

1) The analysand identifies the analyst with a figure in a dream of the analysand.

2) The analyst appears in his or her own person in the dream of the analysand.

3) The analysand appears in a dream of the analyst.

4) There are sexual dreams, by either the analysand or the analyst, about the other person.

There are other possibilities, of course, but these four raise the major questions of technique involved in relating dreams to the transformative field of analysis. Let us consider them more carefully in sequence.

1) *The analysand identifies the analyst with a figure in a dream,* even though the figure is *not* manifestly the analyst. Since in Jungian theory the actions and persons in dreams are not considered to be disguises of reality (as in Freud's view), it is a matter of interpretation to say that a figure in a dream is "really" someone known to the dreamer in waking life. As we shall soon see, even if the analyst actually does appear, it is *still* important to consider whether the dream is speaking

objectively or subjectively. Overinterpretation of dream figures as referring to the analyst may even increase the transference to an unnecessarily dangerous degree, particularly when the dreams have an erotic character. It is generally best to maintain the position that if the dream meant the actual person of the analyst, it would have shown the analyst clearly in the dream. Other figures will reveal the structure of the complexes constellated in the patient, and those figures *may* influence the transference, of course, but they need not do so. The excessive identification of dream images with actual persons constitutes *interpersonal reductionism;* it places undue pressure on the interpersonal sphere of meaning, thereby overemphasizing the transference aspects of the therapeutic situation.

2) *The analyst appears in his own form in a dream of the patient.* In such instances it is more likely that the dream is speaking of the objective situation involving the person of the analyst, although that is by no means certain; the analyst may serve a symbolic function, representing a part of the patient's own psyche (the "inner analyst") based upon interaction with the analyst, a representation that occurs more often after significant changes have occurred in the character of the neurosis. With dreams of this type, there is an additional responsibility for the analyst to objectively assess his relation to the patient, including countertransference reactions, since the patient's dream may be referring to an unconscious aspect of the analyst.

3) *The patient appears in a dream of the analyst.* This should cause the analyst to seriously consider the possibility of countertransference distortions that may impede the therapeutic process. The analysand in the dream may personify a complex of the analyst's that has been constellated in his personal life or within the analytic situation. At the very least, such a dream indicates a need to modify the analyst's conscious view of the patient. Jung mentions a dream in which he saw a female patient as much more of an important person in her own right than he had consciously assessed her to be, a simple correction or compensation of his undervaluing of her on the conscious level.[10]

Should such a dream be discussed with the analysand? From my own experience, the answer is generally "no," although this (like all maxims) is not invariably the right course.

When one discusses the dream of a person with that same person in waking life there is a danger that the person dreamt about will consider the dream to be "deeper" or "more true" than the consciously stated position of the dreamer. It is like offering an unconscious product, which may not be fully understood by the dreamer, as a projection screen for the person to whom the dream is told. Since the patient does not have the same training or experience as the analyst, it is likely that unconscious distortions of his view of the analyst may occur, further increasing the likelihood of difficulties in the transference-countertransference. The same rule applies in general to sharing dreams of a friend with the friend in waking life, although again there are exceptions.

The analyst must understand as far as possible the meaning of his dream of the patient, and relate to the patient out of an increased awareness of what is taking place between them. Thus the ego of the analyst takes responsibility for the dream and its meaning. If the dream is particularly enigmatic, the analyst should arrange a supervision hour with a colleague.

4) *Sexual dreams by either analyst or analysand about the other.* It is particularly important to handle these with the appropriate analytical technique, since the sexualization of the transference-countertransference can lead to unnecessary complications, particularly when (as is rare) it is acted out. The occurrence of sexual dreams on either side should not be surprising, since sexual feelings are natural in any relationship, particularly if there is emotional depth. In his "Tavistock Lectures," Jung suggests that a patient's sexual dreams of the analyst are an attempt to bridge an emotional gap between them.[11] This would seem true of sexual attraction in general— it suggests a potential value in an unknown area of a relationship, a value that is not yet conscious and cannot as yet be clearly specified, although its presence is announced through the sexual attraction. Sexual dreams may also indicate that a transformative process is beginning in the unconscious (of either the analysand, analyst or both), much as in the alchemical drawings that Jung used to illustrate his essay on transference. (The unconscious often makes use of sexual imagery to symbolize non-physical processes of union and transformation, although the waking-ego is inclined to interpret such dreams literally.)

As an example, an analyst dreamed of having sexual intercourse with an attractive female patient. The dream occurred three days before the woman reported a similar dream. There was no conscious awareness of sexual interest by either party, nor were there any seductive or flirtatious remarks or actions by either. The theme did not recur in subsequent dreams of either the analysand or the analyst. The parallel sexual dreams seemed to indicate a new phase of analysis, in which a more transformative tone prevailed and the analysand gained a fresh perspective on the neurotic patterns in her life, which had included repetitive and compulsive sexual affairs.

Medication in Analysis

If the analyst is a physician, dreams may indicate when to initiate or terminate psychotropic drugs as an adjunct treatment to facilitate the analytic process. Non-medical analysts will have similar questions, of course, and may wish to seek consultation on the use of medication. There are purists who would object to the use of any medication during analytical work, but that position is becoming less tenable. The general purpose of analysis is to help the ego come into a responsible relationship with the transformative and individuative process of its own psyche. Wisely used, medication is as likely to be a help as a hindrance in that goal. If medication is used *instead of* analytical work, it is an impediment. If it is used judiciously, so as to allow the ego to work more effectively in analysis, it can be a useful part of the transformative process.

A patient who has too much anxiety (or too little) cannot be sufficiently reflective to move effectively in analysis. The use of one or more of the many tranquilizing medications may be of value. Similarly, if the patient is so depressed that nothing seems of value, including analysis, the use of antidepressant medication can be an essential aid. The goal of any use of medication is to move the patient's ego to the midrange of affective pressure, the range in which neither anxiety nor depression are so overwhelming as to interfere with the work of insight therapy. If the patient is not anxious or depressed *enough,* analysis may also drift aimlessly; but in these instances there is no medication to move the ego toward midrange and the movement must be initiated by either unconscious processes (frequently a dream) or by the analyst arousing sufficient affect through interpretation or exhortation. At times, the addition of concurrent group therapy will evoke the affective responses that are lacking in the one-to-one analytical situation.

Dreams can indicate when medication is needed or when it can safely be discontinued, although they should not be relied upon as a sole criterion. A young man in a schizophrenic process, for example (as previously discussed), had periods of exacerbation when it was necessary to increase the dosage of his antipsychotic medication to avoid the necessity of rehospitalizing him. Several recurring motifs were observed in his dreams just before he began a regressive phase. These included a car rolling backward out of control, animals without skin and destructive dream figures bent on murder and even the destruction of the entire world. When these motifs appeared, his medication was increased, often preventing a period of relapse.

A person who is depressed may continue to report depression even when there is underlying improvement; this is apparently a defense against resuming the responsibilities associated with giving up the role of an ill patient. If dreams take on a more normal appearance, it may be safe to begin the withdrawal of medication, carefully watching for any worsening of the clinical condition. The "normality" of dreams is best judged against knowledge of the patient's dreams prior to the depression, but fairly common motifs that may offer some indication of improvement are a) the absence of symbols of aggression against the dream-ego, and b) absence of symbols referring to periods of the past in which the neurotic conflicts were formed or intensified.

Reductive or Prospective Analysis

Reductive analysis is the term suggested by Jung for the traditional primary emphasis of Freudian psychoanalysis: reducing the current conflict to its supposed origins in the past life of the patient. Such reductive work tends to locate the sufficient cause of the neurosis in a past event, including the past attitude toward the event. Jung never abandoned reductive analysis and felt that it was the appropriate emphasis (at any age) when there were clear indicators that a major component of the neurotic difficulty could be traced to complexes based on past experience. Jung simply relativized reductive analysis, showing it to have a specialized use rather than being the only or necessary way to the alleviation of all neurotic suffering. In contrast to reductive analysis, prospective analysis is more teleologically oriented, asking what the life process is moving *toward* rather than looking at the impediments it has encountered in the past.

In actual analytical practice, there are important occasions for both reductive and prospective analysis. Dreams can be a most sensitive indicator of when to place emphasis on one type of work or the other.

The primary indication that reductive analysis is required occurs in the personal amplifications of dream motifs, both characters and setting. A man with a history of seriously recurring depressions, all of which were triggered by psychodynamic factors associated with environmental changes, tended to dream of his childhood on a poor dirt-farm whenever he was approaching a depression. At other times, when he was more stable, such motifs were rare in his dreams. These motifs indicated a need to deal with his complexes by reductive analysis. Another man, beginning to work through a severe and persistent neurosis, had a series of dreams set in the vicinity of his childhood home, which was symbolic of a fixation to an early experience of the world at about age three. In these dreams there were first images of Mafia-like intrusions into the judicial system of a non-existent town near the childhood home, then dreams of directly leaving the home by airplane (a physical impossibility), and finally a more symbolic image of underground, zombie-like figures emerging from where they had been buried (possibly indicating that they had been buried in the unconscious). Subsequent to this series of dreams, he began to take a different attitude toward the regressive character of his neurotic attachments, foreshadowing a period of improvement marked by a decrease in his neurotic depression.

Conversely, when images from the past are absent from dreams, it seems less important to focus on reductive analysis. Improvement may come more rapidly with a focus on current affective states and their neurotic aspects. Such work may focus on any aspect of the patient's functioning that is affectively charged: the transference-countertransference, involvements with current family or friends, stresses in the work environment, relationships that are observed in group therapy, etc.

The value of dreams becomes particularly apparent in working on current affective problems, for in all these areas *other than* dreams it is important to subtract the outer reality from the patient's descriptions. For example, if there is a marked affective difficulty with someone for whom the patient works, the analyst must allow for the difficulty to be based on the actual nature of the other person rather than upon the distortions of the person by the patient's neurotic perception. Even in assessing affective situations in the transference-countertransference field, it may be difficult for the analyst to be objective enough about himself to recognize his own countertransference contributions to the difficulty. In dreams, however, we are able to begin the inquiry with data that is *already* symbolic. Since the ego does not produce the dream, ego distortions do not have to be taken into account, although one must still be concerned with questions of objective or subjective interpretation of the dream.

The Affect-Ego and Dreams

In his work on the word association experiment, which antedated his first meeting with Freud, Jung clearly defined the nature of a *complex* and of the *affect-ego*. A complex is a group of related ideas and images, held together by a common emotional tone and based upon an archetypal core.[12] In discussing the acute effects of the complex upon consciousness, Jung defined the affect-ego as a modification of the ego resulting from its connection to a strongly toned complex.[13]

The energy associated with a strongly charged complex in the personal unconscious modifies the ego's ability to maintain its usual sense of reality, resulting in an affect-ego state. The ego experiences a loss of its accustomed objectivity, feels the influx of the affect associated with the complex and may have difficulty maintaining the usual boundaries of personal identity.

The creation of an affect-ego state is characteristic of most dreams. Dreams ordinarily have a dramatic structure, with a beginning problem (including setting and cast of characters), a development of the problem, some reaction by the dream-ego (including non-action and emotional reactions) and an outcome. It is important to inquire carefully into the emotional reactions (or lack of them) of the dream-ego, since these as well as actions are a part of the dream-ego's response to the constellated complexes imaged in the other figures of the dream.

If the dream-ego is involved in a very dramatic situation in the dream, but does not show the emotional reaction that would be appropriate if the situation were a waking one, the dream may be indicating a pathological lack of emotional awareness by that particular ego construction. A particularly subtle aspect of the clinical use of dreams is the interpretation of the emotional responsiveness (or its absence) of the dream-ego in relation to the subsequent scenes in the dream. Consider a hypothetical example in which the dream-ego is attacked by another figure but declines to defend itself, trying to make friends with the attacker. This shows a particular ego attitude toward an aggressive content in the psyche. What follows next may show what the unconscious psyche "thinks" of such an ego attitude. It would not be surprising if the attack were renewed with greater energy, suggesting that the dreammaker wishes the dream-ego to become more active in its own behalf.

Another frequent development within a dream occurs if the dream-ego fails to respond adequately to some challenge in the dream (judged by what would be appropriate in the same situation in waking life), and the scene immediately changes to a more serious challenge. For example, the dream-ego is faced with a civil war setting in which a soldier on the other side is firing at the dream-ego, who goes into a cave to avoid the conflict; then the scene changes to one in which the dream-ego is in a body of water and sees shark fins approaching. This sequence suggests that a more serious and primitive threat (the attacking sharks) will appear if the dream-ego attempts to avoid a confrontation on the more human level.

As a general rule, it seems that the closer a conflict in dreams comes to a personal confrontation on a human level, the more likely it is to be approaching a point of possible resolution. Over a series of dreams it is sometimes possible to follow such an evolution in clear progression, from 1) a fight against primitive forces, such as jungle animals, spacemen or large impersonal battle scenes, changing into 2) a more local conflict such as a civil war, which indicates a potential unity of the two warring sides of the psyche, and finally 3) a non-lethal conflict, shown as contained within rules that apply to both sides—for instance an athletic contest or ball game between two teams.

Although one must be cautious in making generalizations, it is at least true to say that conflict motifs in dreams are often associated with the differentiation of the ego from the unconscious, while the more developed images of individuation—such as the alchemical imagery of the *coniunctio,* usually pictured as sexual union or marriage—occur after ego autonomy has been achieved.

The affect-ego in a dream image may be seen at times to correlate with an affective state observed in the waking-ego. When this connection is evident, the dream image of the ego may serve as a shorthand way of referring to the problematic ego state. Analysts and analysands thus often develop a kind of private language using dream images—"You're acting like you did with the Mongol horseman," or "Is this your civil war ego again?" Using dream images for communication in other areas of the patient's life is a very valuable part of the analytic art, although like all techniques it must not be overused.

This use of the basic healing activity of analysis can be pictured as helping the patient to experience various troubling affect-ego states *simultaneously* with an awareness of the containing and nurturing boundary of the analytical relationship, based primarily upon the reality of the conscious relationship between the analyst and the analysand, even though there may be potentially disruptive unconscious conflicts between them. The analyst has the responsibility of maintaining the *temenos* of the analysis (the place, setting, helpful attitude, etc.) and of helping the patient to experience within that safe boundary the disturbing affect-ego states that cause neurotic interference in the life process.

Delayed Interpretation and Non-Interpretation

As the analyst becomes familiar with the use of dreams in clinical practice, some specialized problems may arise. Some patients may use an overabundance of dreams to decoy the analytical process away from areas that need urgent attention. Often, however, the dreams themselves will show a resistance to such a diversion if they are fully and honestly reported.

Occasionally, an analysand brings so many dreams that it is not possible to work with all of them. A selective process is then necessary. The analyst may ask the patient to select the dream with the greatest affective charge (where an affect-ego is most strongly constellated). Often such a dream is the one that the patient least wishes to discuss, since it may contain painful shadow elements or transference problems. If the patient brings all the dreams in a written form, it is often possible for the analyst to scan over the reports and notice motifs that are similar to significant dreams that have already been discussed in analysis; these can then be chosen for the most intensive work. Some dreams may be put aside and kept in mind for possible consideration at a later time. Whenever there is an actual affect-ego state of significant magnitude, the discussion of the material associated with that will properly take precedence over dream interpretation. Such a state might arise in the field of the transference-countertransference, in the patient's daily relationships, at work or elsewhere.

As a general rule, analysis should focus on the most charged affect-ego state, whether that is in waking life or is indicated in a dream. If the affect-ego under consideration occurs in a dream but not in waking life, re-enactment of the dream may evoke it for analysis in the immediate situation. A number of techniques can be utilized for such a purpose: the well-known gestalt technique of asking the person to "be" the dream-ego image, speaking in the first person as if the action were happening in the present; hypnoanalytic and active imagination techniques; group psychotherapy with some use of psychodrama techniques; the simple device of asking the patient to retell the dream from the point of view of one of the characters other than the dream-ego. Any of these techniques may evoke a resurgence of the affect-ego state and permit therapeutic working through of the complex.

When not to interpret a dream is a subtle question of analytical technique. In general there are two major indicators to consider in leaving a dream uninterpreted. The first is when the dream shows something about the patient that the analyst believes is true on the basis of other observations but which the patient seems totally unready to acknowledge. This is the classic situation in psychoanalysis—the analyst knowing something about the patient that the patient is not yet ready to face. In hypnoanalysis, the lack of insight is sometimes covered by temporary amnesia, with instructions that it will be remembered "in time," when the ego is ready to assimilate it.

The second indicator for delaying a dream interpretation is the situation in which the waking-ego needs the affective experience of the dream more than any analytical understanding of it. Such instances are rare but important, and frequently occur when there is a marked need for repair of a damaged ego-image, often because of a low sense of worth dating from childhood. For example, a woman who had experienced severe emotional deprivation from her personal mother had a dream of the Virgin Mary, with a sense of having been loved and cared for by Mary. The dream seemed to be an attempt to have the dream-ego experience the maternal and caring aspect of the archetype of the mother, the side of the archetype that was insufficiently evoked and carried by the personal mother (perhaps because of her own neurotic conflicts). At the time of the dream, the patient was in an unstable situation, with severe depression, and had little emotional support in her family. The dream was not interpreted because the analyst felt she most needed the sense of being affectively cared for in a loving manner. At a later time, this dream was associated with other dreams of mothering figures and made part of the analytical discussion of her ongoing dream series.

Concurrent Group and Individual Therapy

Some Jungian analysts are opposed to mixing group and individual analysis, or even opposed to group treatment on principle, but others (including myself) often find a mixture of individual and group work to be more useful than either approach alone. A group process tends to evoke affect-ego states in an immediate situation, much as do dreams. Also, there is a different constellation of the persona and shadow in the group setting. Many patients feel that acceptance by the analyst offers little relief from oppressive guilt because the analyst is "special," he or she "understands but others wouldn't." A group setting seems to constellate the archetypal sense of a society or family; hence acceptance *by* a group often promotes a greater sense of self-acceptability in the patient.

Good analytic technique requires that any decision about beginning or ending an involvement in group therapy be considered with the same care as questions of beginning or ending individual analysis. Dreams are often a great help in making such decisions. As in deciding on any major change, such as stopping analysis, it is often wise to come to the best conclusion possible on the basis of conscious deliberation, then delay the implementation of the decision until there is time to observe the reaction (if any) in the dream material. Taking a conscious position, even if it is later revised, offers a point of reference in consciousness for the dreams to compensate.

Dreams may indicate the need for more involvement in the group process, and indeed usually do so, often by showing that some important activity in the dream occurs in the presence of group members. At times, however, dreams show that the analysand should refrain from entering a group, perhaps because there is more pressing work to be done on an individual basis. One such dream showed that a neighbor wished the dream-ego to cut down a large hedge, but the dream-ego declined, deciding to plant even more hedges. The dream-ego *then* discovered that there was a vast unexplored area, with many buildings, behind his own backyard, together with even more rented garden space beyond that.

When one member of a therapy group dreams of another, it is often fruitful to bring the dream into the group setting for further work. One woman who had just entered a therapy group had a violent reaction to a woman who had been in the group for some time. She felt that the other woman was "the darling of the group," while she herself would be criticized for almost anything. Her reaction, discussed in an individual analytic session, seemed to indicate severe sibling rivalry problems that had not previously been evident. She then had a dream in which she felt very friendly toward the other woman in her therapy group, a dream that clearly seemed to compensate her conscious reaction. She decided to share the dream with the group and quickly realized, with appropriate emotional insight, that she did feel a sense of kinship with the woman she had initially disliked and feared.

Points to Remember

1. The analytic process takes place within the transformative field of the transference-countertransference.
2. It is impossible for the analyst's unconscious processes not to be involved, but they should be a small factor in comparison to those in the analysand.
3. Dreams in which the analysand clearly dreams of the analyst (or vice versa) should be treated with particular care, especially if they contain strongly erotic elements.
4. Dreams can provide clues to the need for reductive or prospective analysis, the use of medication and other clinical choices, but they should only be part of the decision process.
5. Dream interpretation is not always the primary focus of analysis.
6. In general, follow the material associated with the strongest affect-ego state in the analysand.
7. The transformative field of analysis consists of the experience of affect-ego states within the safe *temenos* of the analysis. Maintenance of the safety of the *temenos*, when threatened with disruption, takes precedence over dream interpretation and other aspects of analytical work.
8. The meaning of a dream is never exhausted, even if it seems completely understood. A sense of humbleness is vital in dream interpretation.

6

Ego-Images and Complexes in Dreams

The changes occurring to the dream-ego, the ego-image in the dream, offer many indicators for the clinical course of Jungian analysis. It is again important to remember that the dream must be carefully amplified and then placed in the context of the patient's current life and stage of individuation.

The basic structural concepts of analytical psychology have already been discussed—the identity structures of ego and shadow and the more relational structures of the persona and the anima/animus. Dream images often can readily be assigned to these structural concepts, but it would be a mistake to think such identification in any way sufficed for the clinical use of a dream. The dream is more subtle than any theoretical model of the psyche, which must not be used in such a reductive way. Nevertheless, when employed with proper restraint and with respect for the movement of the dreams, Jung's structural concepts can be a helpful means of psychological orientation for both analyst and patient, and an aid in understanding the immediate task at hand.

Identification of Complexes

Complexes can be identified easily in many dreams, but dreams give more information than merely identifying complexes; they also show *what the psyche is doing* with the constellated complexes. Any unstructured stimulus to which a person free-associates will reveal whatever complexes are constellated at that time. Jung noted this in his work with the word association experiment; his objection to the Freudian technique of free association was simply that it would lead to complexes but would not reveal their relation to the dream images that were the beginning of the associational chain. Since Jung did not believe in the idea of a hidden or "latent" dream meaning behind the manifest dream (which he took as symbolic but not disguised), he did not try to see behind the "disguise" of the dream images; rather, these images were amplified on personal, cultural and archetypal levels to reveal their meaning through other images found naturally associated with them in the mind of the patient.

As well as identifying complexes, a dream may show their unexpected linkage to other complexes. For example, a young woman who had been recently divorced dreamed:

> I am in the house of my former husband, my own old house. It is late at night. I'm in my old bedroom when I hear voices outside. I see my former husband and his new girlfriend. I thought I had told him I'd be staying in the house so that he wouldn't be there. They come up the stairs to go to bed together and go into his bedroom. I realize to my surprise that I am actually in my old bedroom at my parents' house and that my former husband and his girlfriend have gone into my parents' bedroom.

The dream startled her with its suggestion that her feelings for her former husband had an oedipal overtone, putting him in the place of her father. The surprise was even greater because she realized that such an unconscious linkage could account for her sexual aversion to her former husband, an attitude that had contributed to their divorce.

Another patient found a similar connection between a current situation and past feelings about her mother (carried in the mother complex), in two dreams on the same night, while she was working through a severe problem of scrupulosity that had dominated her life for a number of years. Note that the connection to the mother complex is not evident in the first dream, but when that dream is put beside the second dream the mother complex becomes clearly visible:

> *Dream 1:*
> I was on a ledge with three or four other persons and was frightened. I slipped and fell twenty or thirty feet to the ground. When I hit I just lay there to be sure I was all right, but I hoped that people wouldn't think I was just trying to get attention.

> *Dream 2:*
> I was on the roof of my mother's house. Other people were there. I was afraid to jump down. Nobody seemed concerned.

The two dreams have a similar though slightly different

initial image, which serves to link them to the same pattern of complexes, although showing slightly different views of the complex structure. The ledge in the first dream is analogous to the roof of her mother's house in the second dream. In the first dream there is an unintentional fall, followed by an ego state in which the dream-ego's legitimate concern for its own health is put aside in favor of the neurotic thought that it wouldn't look right—"I hoped that people wouldn't think I was just trying to get attention." In the second dream she does not fall, while other people are unconcerned about her precarious position, and her location on "the roof of my mother's house" indicates that the current difficulty arises in a parental complex rather than in the conscious concern to be scrupulous. In a sense, the feeling that she is "too sinful" is compensated (or shown in a more true light) by her being inappropriately "too high up" and in an awkward place—the ledge or roof. She linked the concern with the family with her disappointment that little attention had been shown to her recent newborn son, in contrast to the attention she felt had been showered on her sister's first child.

Structural Shifts: Borders and Boundaries

Shifts from one ego-identity to another may be symbolized in dreams, frequently taking the form of crossing a border or boundary, or passing over a body of water on a bridge. Such imagery shows two contrasting states of being and the ability of the ego to move from one to the other as a basis for its identity. This is a contrast to the more neurotic movements from one identity to another *within* a stable neurotic pattern. Of course, if the stable pattern is neurotic, a shift of identity entirely away from the pattern translates as clinical improvement, although the movement of identity away from *any* familiar pattern causes anxiety until the new pattern is stabilized.

A man spoke harshly to a woman in his group therapy session, something he was not accustomed to do as he usually hid his negative feelings, which kept his shadow hidden but also prevented its coming into consciousness for possible integration. He felt badly about having expressed his negative feelings and was tempted to withdraw into the old pattern of keeping things to himself and thereby freezing himself in a neurotic and unchanging state. Immediately after the group therapy experience he dreamed:

> I am at a boundary, something like the Berlin wall but it was in Poland. I was on the free side but for some reason I wanted to go into the un-free side of the boundary where I might be caught and unable to return. I had to be careful. There were no people around and I was frightened.

In addition to referring to his tendency to cross into an "un-free" identity because of his guilt, the dream led him to reflect upon an impulse to begin an affair with a woman he had known before his marriage. The "free" versus "un-free" aspects of his personality could be correlated with his basic neurotic problem and its manifestation in many areas of his life.

Relational and Identity Structures

The psychological structures identified by Jung can be a useful tool in understanding dreams: persona, shadow, anima and animus, Self and other archetypal images, and of course the various forms and roles of the ego. These are not often used in talking with patients about dreams, unless the patient introduces them, but they are helpful in orienting the therapist. Their excessive use in ordinary discussions with the analysand runs a grave risk of promoting intellectual understanding at the expense of real emotional insight and transformation. When the analysand is also an analyst-in-training, the identification of the structural components in his or her material may be a useful teaching device, but should be done only after the affective understanding has been accomplished.

The Persona

Persona roles are often thought of as "masks" and given a negative meaning in contrast to the "true" personality experienced by the ego ("I just want to be myself"); however, this is a misunderstanding of the function of the persona. The persona is simply a structure for relating to the collective conscious situation, analogous to the concept of role in social theory. The ego usually knows it can identify with or disidentify from persona roles, while it is generally not aware that it can also identify or not with shadow identities, which seem to be a part of the ego but unacceptable. The persona seems optional, the shadow seems compulsive, although both are simply ego-identity roles that are held in different tensions in relation to the other structural components of the psyche.

In dreams, persona aspects are often shown by clothing (which can be taken on or off) and by roles, such as playing a part in a drama. Identification with the persona may lead the ego to feel that it is empty and "dead" without the role to play. This was strikingly evident in the dream of an army officer who found himself off-stage and dead in his uniform, while everyone else who had been on stage was going to other parts of their lives. Conversely, the absence of suitable clothing, or being naked in a social setting, is a dream motif that seems to indicate an inadequate persona.

When it functions well, the persona simply facilitates the activity of the ego in social interaction. The persona is also a vehicle for the transformation of the ego: unconscious contents may first be experienced through a persona role and then later integrated into the ego as part of its own tacit functional identity. If one takes a simple enough example, such as learning to play the piano, this movement from persona to tacit ego structure is quite clear. One first practices playing the piano, exerting great effort, and then at some point the skill becomes automatic and unconscious, although it can be recalled for conscious review if there is difficulty.

When the persona is identified in a dream, therefore, it must be looked at in relation to the other structures represented in the dream and seen in the perspective of the overall dream movement. The persona is not, in itself, positive or negative.

The Shadow

Shadow images also seem to carry a sense of being negative, although as mentioned earlier this too can be an illusion based upon the original dissociation of the shadow contents from the immature ego in childhood. The child has little of the adult's autonomy and can dissociate a perfectly good part of the ego into the structure of the shadow in conformity to a family or social situation that is itself neurotic (or simply expressing a transient reality situation in the family). If the shadow identity is not later brought into consciousness for revision, the traits in the shadow are not easily available to the ego for its normal functioning. Any type of psychotherapy is to some extent involved in bringing the shadow into consciousness and making a more adult decision as to its suitability for inclusion into the dominant ego-identity. If shadow integration is not achieved, the shadow contents tend to be projected onto others (usually of the same sex as the ego) and offer irrational impediments to easy interpersonal functioning.

The dream of a physician who had many immature problems showed both shadow and persona qualities and the relationship between these two components of his psyche:

> I was an undercover agent [hidden identity] up against the German Gestapo [symbol of a collective shadow]. The uniform I was wearing had the wrong bottoms on it [persona problem]. Three or four men were trying to help me find the right bottoms for the uniform [possibly helpful parts of the shadow].

During the day preceding the dream, this man had seen a television program about hunting for missing Nazis. He considered Gestapo persons as "evil people, misfits, crazy people with authority, rigid, dogmatic, constrictive." These associations described, to some degree, his own shadow, but also expressed his fear of dealing with such material. The dream showed that the inadequate persona (the not-quite-right uniform) and the serious nature of the shadow problems were related.

The shadow may contain qualities that need to be integrated for a more comprehensive ego structure. This is frequently seen in dreams of an aggressive shadow figure that is needed to compensate an overly passive waking-ego, although the reverse configuration may also be seen—a shadow figure of a more gentle or compliant nature than the waking-ego.

Anima/Animus

The anima or animus primarily serves the function of enlarging the personal sphere, which includes the inner "space" of ego, persona and shadow as well as that of the anima and animus. This is often accomplished through projection onto a figure of the opposite sex in the outer world, but it may also occur through the mediation of such a figure in dreams and fantasies. Fairytales are a rich source of anima and animus images. Excessive reliance on the activity of the anima (in a man) or the animus (in a woman) impoverishes the ego. In waking life, the presence of the anima or animus is usually evident when an emotion or thought is held with some emotional tenacity but in an impersonal manner. Feelings and opinions that are couched in terms of "ought" or "should"— based on collective, generalized rules of acceptable behavior or male and female stereotypes—often come from the unconscious parts of the persona or from the anima/animus. This can be recognized precisely because the quality of the feeling or opinion is impersonal; it may be directed toward another person, but there is no discrimination between the actuality of that other person and the projected fantasy of what he or she "should" be.

In the process of withdrawing projections of the anima or animus the personal ego is enlarged, increasing the range of consciousness. Failure to withdraw a projection onto, for example, a loved one, may lead to an embittered and shallow relationship—the former loved one does not live up to expectations, he or she is found to be not the person the projection promised. If the projection is withdrawn and its contents made part of the subjective world of the projecting ego, there may still be room for a good personal relationship with the person who was previously seen largely in terms of the projection.

The dreams of two women show an excessive reliance upon the animus, rather than developing needed strength in the ego itself. The first woman dreamed that she was descending a long staircase in a ballet class, using certain ballet steps. A man came to help. He carried her down the staircase while she tried to make her feet move as though she were actually dancing down the stairs herself. She reported, "It was quite an effort to move my feet so quickly, since there were so many tiny little stairs, and I'm not sure I really kept up as I was carried down."

The second woman dreamed that she was fishing in a boat with her father when something was caught on the line. Although it was her line, her father reeled in the fish, seeming to use all his strength. For some time she resisted the thought that she was relying too much on the figure of the father as animus, focusing rather on the interpretation that the dream showed her father "finally" doing something for her. She was an exceptionally intelligent and creative woman who doubted unnecessarily her own abilities—that is, the abilities were present but unconscious (in the animus), not integrated into the tacit functional structure of the ego.

In the classical view, as previously pointed out, the anima tended to be associated with the unconscious feeling of a man, while the animus was identified with the underdeveloped thinking of a woman. These shorthand generalizations were perhaps true in traditional European culture, in which Jung spent his formative years, but they can be decidedly untrue in any individual case, in which the configuration of the anima or animus is determined by the organizational structure of the personal sphere and the contents assigned to the persona and shadow while growing up.

One man beginning a new stage of anima development in which his idealized feelings of women were less projected onto actual women in the environment dreamed that he caught a fleeting glimpse of a ghostly woman, laughing and singing as she moved across a hallway toward a garden. This seemed to show the anima as separable from his projections and as in a sense connected to the past (ghost-like).

Although the anima and the animus are generally contra-sexual to the gender identity of the ego, there are certainly clinical instances where they are contaminated with the shadow, and the sex of the anima or animus is thus less certain. If there is identity confusion in the sex role of the ego, there may be a reflection of this confusion in the dream images of the shadow and anima or animus. It must be remembered, too, that these structural terms are to some degree generalizations; the actual dreams and dream images are more complex than the concepts.

The Self and the Ego-Self Axis

The Self, the regulating center of the psyche, may also appear in dreams, along with other archetypal images. Appearances of the Self, the archetypal core of the ego, often indicate a need for stabilization of the ego, since there tends to be a reciprocal relationship between the stability of the ego and the Self manifesting in a stable form. If the ego is confused and in disarray, the Self is more likely to appear in a very ordered form, such as a mandala. Psychologically speaking, a mandala image is one that emphasizes the totality of something, usually showing quite clearly a periphery and a center. In its historical sense, the term mandala refers to certain very structured meditation symbols used in Buddhism, often consisting of a fourgated square or circular city with a central image (to be meditated on) and lesser images surrounding it.

In dreams, the Self imagery may be more inexact, as a building that surrounds a central courtyard with a fountain, or even two large buildings joined by a central common wing. The Self may appear as a voice, like the "voice of God," that seems to come from "everywhere" and generally has a sense of unquestioned integrity and correctness, seeming to simply state things as they actually are, with no room for disagreement. A classic example is the dream already referred to, consisting entirely of one sentence—an authoritative voice saying "You are not leading your true life!"

It is impossible to construct a list of possible images of the Self, since virtually *any* image that appears with sufficient dignity and meaning may carry the force of this central archetype. Also, it is important to distinguish between the archetype of the Self and any particular archetypal image of the Self that appears in dreams. As archetype, the Self is the ordering center of the psyche as a whole, a whole greater than the ego but related most intimately to the ego. The Self as the totality of the psyche is the generative field of the individuation process. But the Self is also the archetypal pattern on which the development of the ego is based. Conceptually, the centering quality of the total psyche is the Self, while the centering quality of consciousness (and of the personal sphere) is the ego. When we speak of the Self in dreams, we are actually considering it as an archetypal image of the orderliness of the psyche as a whole. Any archetypal image of the Self in dreams is an image of this totality as seen from the point of view of a particular dream-ego. As the contents of the ego shift, so may the image of the Self, although the relationship between them always remains that of the center of conscious-ness (ego) to the center of the psyche (Self).

The *ego-Self axis* is a term sometimes used to describe the relationship between the ego and the Self. There are some objections to this term, primarily to the static quality implied by the word "axis." The actual relationship of ego and Self is more shifting and varied. Personally I prefer the term *ego-Self spiration* (from Latin *spirare,* to breathe), which emphasizes the breathing-like, back-and-forth flow between the ego and the Self.

In his autobiography, Jung relates two of his own dreams to illustrate the essentially enigmatic relationship between ego and Self. In one of the dreams, Jung realized that he himself was being projected by a flying saucer, not the other way around. In the second, Jung felt himself to be a dream figure in the dream of a meditating yogi who also had the face of Jung. "I knew that when he awakened, I would no longer be."[14]

This movement or potential movement between ego and Self can be seen in dreams that emphasize the ego-image being observed by or dependent upon something larger and more powerful than itself. For example, a man in his mid-forties dreamed he was on a Sea Scout cruise and fell over-board while roughhousing with his friends. As he began to swim back to the boat, it changed into a large ocean liner. He then stopped because he heard a strange sound. He realized it was a large whale some seventy or eighty feet beneath the surface. For a moment he "saw" himself on the surface of the ocean as if he were the whale. His surface form looked like "no more than a waterbug." He felt a sense of alertness, as if something momentous might happen, but there was no fear and the large whale was not particularly threatening.

Here the dreamer's somewhat adolescent ego-identity (Sea Scout), when it comes into contact with the unconscious (ocean), suddenly becomes aware that it is, in a sense, the object of a superordinate subject (the whale). Simultaneously, the former carrier of the dream-ego (the small boat) becomes a large ocean liner. The ego-image in contact with the water, therefore, experiences itself as between two points of view that are both larger than itself—the whale in the ocean and the man-made liner on the surface. The adolescent (*puer*) attitude is being gently compensated and something awesome, but not threatening, seems about to happen.

Archetypal Amplification

Archetypal images in dreams often indicate a change of course in ego development or compensate an inadequately formed ego structure. Since there is an archetypal core behind every complex, it is always possible to amplify any motif in the direction of its archetypal foundations. Archetypal amplification, however, should be used with restraint in the clinical setting. An unwanted and even dangerous side effect of excessive archetypal amplification is fascination with unconscious images and their archetypal meanings. This fascination can lead one away from the process of individuation, which requires finding a personal meaning among the many archetypal possibilities offered both in the unconscious and in the outer collective world. (Indeed, some persons present themselves proudly for Jungian analysis, believing that their already close waking contact with what Jung called archetypes is an eminent "qualification," only to later realize—if they do —that it is their major problem. An *undifferentiated* wholeness is still unconsciousness.)

As a practical matter, the analyst is only able to interpret those archetypal images that can be identified as such. This depends largely upon a broad familiarity with mythology, folklore and religion, repositories of significant images that have been meaningful enough to a sufficiently wide range of people to have been carried over extended periods of time and embedded in written traditions.

At times there are dream images that can be amplified meaningfully only with archetypal associations.[15] More often, the archetypal images are quite evident in cultural forms that are familiar. In the following dream, for instance, there are a number of images and motifs that can be considered from an archetypal perspective: turtle (symbol of totality, foundation of the world); egg (symbol of original beginnings, the cosmic egg); the mysterious movement from "one" to "two"; the connection of infant offspring to mother; and the mysterious voice that speaks unquestioned truths.

I saw a shiny turtle shell on the beach. There was a bird egg nearby and it too was shiny like the turtle shell. A disembodied voice spoke and said, "It looks like an egg but if you hold it in your hand it will be two eggs." The voice sounded professional and god-like. I picked up the egg and mysteriously it was two eggs. The voice said they will both hatch and there will be a mother bird and a baby bird and the baby will find its way to the mother. Then I immediately saw the baby bird stumbling on the beach toward the mother.

In spite of the many archetypal possibilities for amplification, this dream was left embedded within the series of dreams in which it occurred, with no special emphasis. It might have been interpreted in terms of the archetypal development of the mother-child relationship (the one egg becomes two, one the child, the other the mother), with any number of embellishments from religion and mythology. But the effect of the dream itself was enough to move the dreamer toward the resolution of a deep difficulty with the image of the mother, affecting both her relationship to her personal mother (which became less problematical) and her relationship to her own role as mother of her children (which also improved). Within a short time there was another dream which showed that she must quickly clear away unnecessary "scaffolding" around a building in order to prevent a dangerous explosion. This seemed to the analyst to confirm his decision not to amplify the earlier dream, feeling that the purpose or message of the dream was better dealt with on a more personal level, and in any case had already been heard.

7

Common Dream Motifs

It is not possible to present an encyclopedic list of dream motifs and their usual meanings. To attempt to do so would be to move in the direction of a "cookbook" of dream interpretations, which would be misleading as well as inappropriate.

All dream images are contextual. The same image may mean different things in different dreams of the same person, and certainly so when it is dreamed by someone else. The experienced therapist realizes that any discussion of motifs cannot in principle be exhaustive, but serves only to exemplify a style and possibilities of interpretation that *may* be useful in entirely different contexts. Personal analysis and supervision of one's own cases by a skilled dream interpreter with a background in depth psychology remain the most direct and practical ways to learn how to work clinically with dreams.

The examples presented here should therefore be taken as no more than illustrative of specific cases that may give clues to other cases, which will always differ in their particular details and meaning.[16]

Incest

The appearance of incest in dreams is not necessarily a negative sign. Prior to crossing the Rubicon and marching on Rome, Caesar had a dream of incest with his mother, a dream that was interpreted (correctly, most likely) as indicating that "Mother" Rome would receive him happily and not resist. In ancient Egypt incest between royal siblings was considered appropriate, if not actually required, reflecting the brother-sister incest inherent in the archetypal myth of Isis and Osiris. Incest in a dream may represent a contact of the dream-ego with the archetypal meaning personified by a parent or sibling, a contact that may result in some exceptional movement away from fixation points in the personal areas of the psyche. Similarly, incest with a sibling of the same sex often indicates the need for the dreamer to assimilate unconscious shadow qualities—or shows that it is already happening.

On the negative side, incest motifs involving the parents may suggest that a maternal or paternal imago lies behind more personal complexes and interferes with the achievement of the *coniunctio,* the balanced pairing of male and female elements, often expressed in sexual imagery. For example, a man who had experienced difficulties in many relationships with women since his divorce from a cold and controlling wife dreamed that he met his own mother when she was about fifty years of age (he at the time was in his mid-fifties). He embraced his mother and as he did so he felt her vagina vibrating with sexual energy. It did not bother him in the dream, but when he awoke he was disturbed.

That dream helped to identify an incestuous element in his relationships with women; additionally, it was an aid in recognizing the madonna/prostitute split in his psyche, based partially on the overidealization of his mother, whom he considered non-sexual.

Mourning

Mourning processes seem to appear naturally in dreams. In uncomplicated bereavement, the dead loved one may appear as if alive, the frequency of the dreams gradually decreasing (and their symbolic content often increasing) as the mourning process moves to a healthy conclusion, usually within six to eight months after the death. In cases of prolonged and pathological mourning, where the survivor is unable or unwilling to accept the death of the loved person, the dream images often show the deceased in a negative light, or as if the deceased is trying to abandon the dream-ego.

For example, a woman with severe parental difficulties went through a prolonged and difficult mourning after the suicide of her husband, the only person to whom she had felt close emotionally. Many dreams showed that he was actually dead, that she should not try to follow him in death, that there was no room for her to be buried next to him, etc. One of the last of these dreams, several years after his death, occurred even after she had remarried (not too successfully).

In the dream she was divorced from her dead husband and he had another wife. The dream-ego wanted a child, but her husband had a vasectomy (which he had not had in real life). He went to have it undone, but they did it again anyway. Then the dream-ego was to have the vasectomy, but the surgeon pointed out that she had no testicles. She and her husband agreed that the seashore where they were was not as attractive as that on their honeymoon. A large wave, two stories high, was approaching and in it was "a red-skinned thing" like "inside a female body," which reminded the dream-ego of a dream long ago about such a sea creature.

The dream contains several motifs which indicate that clinging to the marriage is unrealistic, even dangerous: the husband is divorced and remarried, there is no possibility for children (new developments between them), there is a threatening wave (unconscious contents), etc.

Houses

Houses commonly appear in dreams as images of the psyche. Many times there are unknown rooms in the house, indicating hidden or unexplored areas of the patient's potential ego structure. Distinctions between parts of a house may be symbolically important: the cellar, the attic, the roof, balconies, bedrooms, etc. Kitchens, for instance, are a place of transformation of raw food into cooked dishes; in dreams they sometimes have the character of the alchemical laboratory, a place of more profound transformations. Bathrooms in dreams may refer to "elimination" or the difficulty in "letting go." Sometimes the mere setting of the dream action in a certain house from the past allows inferences as to the origin of the complexes involved.

The house itself may stand for various parts of the ego-structure, as in the dream of a man beginning to experience a sense of freedom as his excessive, neurotic self-criticism waned:

> I was looking for a house. The scene was like west Texas, with wide horizon and broad sky. A beautiful day. I went up to a house that was on several acres. It was a used, comfortable house, with a swimming pool. I walked around it looking at it.

In the same session in which he reported this dream he described a changed feeling in his everyday life. Although the change was not spontaneously associated with the dream, it had much the same affective tone, suggesting that the tacit structure of the ego, as reflected in the dream, was also being experienced as a more relaxed emotional state in his ordinary life. He described himself as more stable, less aggressive sexually and otherwise, not disliking his wife as much and feeling that he was not functioning so much on the basis of what he thought others wanted of him. He also felt a change in his relationship with other people, because "I no longer have to *prove* something."

Automobiles

Automobiles and other modes of travel are other images that seem to indicate ego structure or the way in which the ego moves through the various activities of life. The difference between walking and riding in an automobile is a significant symbolic change, as is the distinction between one's own car and the collective nature of a bus. Trains, in contrast to automobiles and buses, are set on a fixed track, without the option of moving somewhat at will; they therefore tend to be associated with compulsive or habitual activities. Closely related to automobiles are streets and highways, where distinctions must be noted between sizes of streets or freeways, whether the dream-ego is moving in the direction of traffic or against or across the flow, difficulties in finding an entrance to a desired pathway, as well as curbs, gutters, potholes, etc.

The contextual nature of dream symbols is nowhere more evident than in all these variations on the theme of transportation. The automobile can even stand for self-esteem (a point that advertisers have not overlooked). For example, a young woman dreamed:

> While driving through an underground parking lot I broadsided another car. Then I went out and bought a *really* small car. Then I realized that I didn't *want* to give up my old car.

In discussing the dream, she linked the imagery to an habitual way of handling stress in a less than effective manner. When she felt that she had made a mistake, she wanted to "run away or clean the slate." "I'm not very self-accepting," she admitted. The dream seemed an opportunity to realize that self-rejection for mistakes and accidents was not necessary.

A major symbolic meaning of an automobile in a dream hinges upon whether it belongs (or in the past belonged) to the dreamer, or whether it is someone else's. A similar significance attaches to the position of the dream-ego within the automobile. The most appropriate position would generally be the driver's seat, from where one is able to determine the course and speed and direction of movement. If the dream-ego is not shown in the driving position, it is important to note who *is* in control of the car (sometimes it is no one). Where does the dream-ego sit? Behind the driver? In the front seat but on the passenger's side? Somewhere else? Between other figures? Outside the car? Remembering that the Self, in making the dream, places the dream-ego in a particular position in the opening scene, one can gain a great deal of information from such a simple matter as the initial seating arrangement within an automobile.

It is difficult to overemphasize the symbolic importance of such apparently insignificant details in dreams. Patients often will not spontaneously report such details, assimilating the memory of the dream to how it "ought" to appear rather than describing the way it was actually presented to the dream-ego. Careful inquiry is always important, but to let the patient fill in the dream details as to what "probably" was there would be like filling in a medical laboratory report with what "probably should" appear when there is no data. Dreams are so unique and individual in their relation to the waking-ego that it is better to clearly know that one has *no* data about a particular motif, than to think one has a true image from the dream when it is really an interpolation from the waking-ego of the dreamer. Patients who add, on inquiry, such "probable" details are trying to be helpful, but they do not appreciate the exquisite specificity of the dream.

Alcohol and Drugs

Images of alcohol and drug use appear in dreams particularly when there is some waking problem with them. Chemical addictions are notoriously difficult to treat by psychological means, and usually require more "primitive" techniques such as group pressure and support. (Unfortunately such approaches are often successful in terms of the addiction but interfere with a finer understanding of psychological processes, as if all one's problems could be solved by abstaining from alcohol or drugs.) But when dreams are followed closely, it is sometimes possible to see the unconscious ready for a change in the addiction pattern—suggesting, supporting or even pushing for one—before any steps are taken by the waking-ego.

A man who had been a non-drinking alcholic for many years decided to allow himself an occasional "harmless" glass of wine with friends. His dreams on two such occasions clearly disapproved, as they did when he allowed himself to take a pain medication that had not been prescribed for him. Another man whose alcohol consumption had slowly and insidiously increased, dreamed almost a year before he decided to face the possibility of alcoholism that such a move was needed —the motif being the loss of his automobile associated with alcohol intake. Still later, with the alcohol problem not yet resolved, he dreamed that his ring finger and the wedding band on it had shrunk to half size, which he interpreted as showing him to be "not the man I should be." In the same series of dreams, a black woman played up to him sexually in order to sell him a pint of milk that did not need refrigeration for $6.85, which he felt might refer to pints of bourbon. The woman in the dream had no real interest in him, only in selling the apparently overpriced milk.

A woman making a valiant attempt to abstain from alcohol reported two dreams on the same night, both of which she associated with her struggle not to drink. In the first dream her purse (feminine identity) was lost, submerged in water (unconscious), but she found it and everything was intact although wet. The "wet" she related to "drying out" from alcohol. In the second dream she was lost in a suburb, but knew she could find her way home, again a good prognostic sign for the eventual successful outcome of her resolve not to drink.

An impressive example is the case of a man in his midthirties whose heavy use of marijuana had dulled his judg-

ment and damaged his marriage. Soon after he entered analysis he had a series of dreams in which crowds held up large
signs and even billboards, proclaiming: DON'T SMOKE
DOPE.

Death

Death in dreams—including murder and the loss of relationships—must be carefully considered in context, for the death
of dream figures seldom refers to actual death; rather it points
to the profound archetypal process of transformation.

A man wrestling with notable oedipal problems was unable
to date comfortably, although he had no difficulty dealing
responsibly and assertively in his business relationships. As he
began to improve, he was particularly proud of a situation in
which he and his brother were with two women. The brother
went into a bedroom with his date, but the analysand, although he felt pressure in the situation to do so, did not really
want to have intercourse with the woman he was with. He was
able to honestly tell her his feelings, a victory for him in terms
of asserting his independence from a collective "macho" belief
that men are always sexually aggressive, a so-called norm that
he had in any case honored more in fantasy than in actuality.

As he was experiencing a sense of freedom from the compulsive oedipal roles, he had two separate dreams in which he
murdered his parents. Now, patricide and matricide are truly
repulsive crimes, but in the context of dreams that occur in
the midst of a dynamic process they can symbolize an alteration in the inner parental imagos, as seemed to be the case
here. The first dream shows quite dramatically how an image
"killed" in a dream may reappear in a transformed state:

> I killed my father who was threatening me. I held him under
> water until he drowned. Later in the dream he was still there
> but no longer a threat to me. Then he came along with me in a
> helpful manner.

The figure in the dream did not look like his actual father, a
clue to its identification as a personification of a personal
complex. In associations, he described his father as a man who
was "emotionless, stubbornly close-minded, but stable." In the
second dream he killed his mother, but when awake he
"didn't remember" any details.

In general, the death of parental imagos in dreams points to a radical change in the oedipal structure of complexes that regularly interfere with the achievement of a firm personal standpoint. When the dream-ego itself does the "killing," it may show the degree to which the dreamer is actively involved in his or her own process.

Snakes

Snakes appear in dreams in many forms that exemplify the wide archetypal meanings that can be carried by a single type of image. Snakes can of course be given a phallic meaning (or even literally associated with the penis), but that is only a part of their symbolic potency. Jung considered that snakes could at times represent the autonomic nervous system, an interesting notion in light of recent brain research that refers to the core of the human brain stem as the "reptilian brain" (in contrast to the more elaborated mammalian brain and the uniquely human expansion of the cerebral cortex).

Snakes often seem to represent simply instinctual energy, particularly when they are present in large numbers, as in the previously mentioned dream of snakes writhing about the sidewalks of a college but not actually on the walkways, which were safe. The serpent can be associated with wisdom; with healing (as on the staff of Asclepius, the physician's emblem); with poison and danger; with proving oneself (as in snake-handling cults); or even as a prefiguration of a much higher value—as the brazen serpent lifted up in the wilderness in the Old Testament was seen as a prefiguration of Christ.

These multiple possible meanings (and there are many others) show the richness and multifaceted nature of archetypal images. In any particular case, it is important to discover a more discrete and personal meaning from the patient's own associations; this avoids the archetypal reductionism of arbitrarily reading in only one of the possible meanings (or reading in too many).

A priest, for example, dreamed that he visited a museum and saw a stuffed snake in a simulated natural setting. The scene then changed and he was holding a large rattlesnake behind the head so that it could not bite him. But it whirled and turned, frightening him, and he let go of it, an act of panic that increased the actual danger of the situation. These two scenes already suggest a conflict with whatever is symbolized by the serpent, because they show the same content at a safe remove from the dream-ego (the stuffed snake in the museum) and also at a closer and more frightening range (when he is holding an actual live snake). His personal association was to having a puffing adder as a "pet" when he was eighteen years old. This led into a stream of associations about masturbation, suggesting that the serpent in this case would be most appropriately taken in its phallic meaning, but with strong ambivalence about sexuality.

The same patient had difficulty dealing with a box of rubber snakes when working on a sandtray projection. He remembered that he had had to refrain from masturbation for two months before he would allow himself to tell anyone that he wished to enter the priesthood, and abstained for an entire year before a critical examination in the seminary. He recalled that his father spoke of abstinence from masturbation as "an angelic virtue." Once he told his novitiate master, with fear and trembling, that he had masturbated in the shower (the master simply said, "Forget it").

Here it can be seen that the snake dream brought to the forefront conflicts that were to a large degree internally generated. In analysis the dream was not interpreted at any length, but was used as a springboard into the discussion of his persisting sexual conflicts.

8

The Dream Frame

In most dreams the frame of the dream does not come into question. Usually the dream is obviously one type of experience and waking life another, so that the dream is simply remembered, analyzed and put into the waking context as a compensation from the unconscious to the existing waking attitude. At times, however, the dream itself raises the question of the correct framework for its understanding. This occurs in two major instances: 1) the dream-within-a-dream, and 2) when one dreams of things "exactly" as they appear in reality. The question is also raised by references in dreams to time and space, and by synchronistic phenomena.

Dream-within-a-Dream

In a dream-within-a-dream, since one dreams that one is dreaming, an "awakening" may occur within the dream. The most complex instance I have seen was a dream in which the dream-ego "awoke" to a "waking state" to find itself (dream-ego number two) still in the dream, awoke from that into another "waking state" (dream-ego number three) and from that into actual waking life.

The dream-within-a-dream shows changes in the tacit ego structure that are more complex than usual. Each "waking-ego" that is within the sleeping and dreaming state shows, it seems, a possible integration that can be lived out by the dreamer without coming fully to terms with the direct relationship between the dream-ego and the waking-ego. It is like a mask over a mask, so that the first unveiling does not reveal the true ego. Classical Freudian theory considered that dreams were disguised, so that a dream of a dream might logically be thought to be an undisguised version of the hidden "latent" dream; such an interpretation would follow the rules of grammatical structure, where a double negative statement becomes a positive assertion. There is no similar Jungian "formula" for handling the dream-within-a-dream, but such shifts within a dream can be seen as movements of various ego-organizations, some of which claim for themselves the status of full waking consciousness, although the complicated dream structure reveals them to be only partial integrations.

To some degree, the dream-within-a-dream is a more complicated form of the frequent shift from scene to scene within a single dream. In the dream-within-a-dream it is as if the action shifts from one entire "stage" to another, so that the first dream seems to have taken place upon a smaller stage that is contained within the larger stage of the next dream. In the usual phenomenology of dreams, however, scene changes take place upon the same "stage."

Interpretation of this complicated dream structure must be carefully undertaken and no set approach is always appropriate. Such dreams tend to exemplify a truth that is seldom appreciated: the process of individuation in its fine structure resembles the creation of a "new world," not just a revision of the ego within the old existing world. It is not only the ego that changes—the entire structure of "world" alters, including the role of significant other persons. This is the reason why when one spouse undertakes analysis, the other is often frightened that it will mean the end of the relationship—and it may if there is movement in one person and not the other, or if the person in analysis mistakenly identifies the old world with the spouse, a psychologically simpler (but usually less valuable) solution than the emergence of a larger world in which the old world is contained and relativized.

Dreams of Reality-as-it-is

The dream frame is also called into question when one dreams of reality "exactly as it is." If the dream is of an actual traumatic situation, of course, the exact duplication is likely to be for the purpose of eventual mastery of what overwhelmed the ego in the original traumatic event. The usual dreams of reality-as-it-is, however, do not arise in connection with traumatic events, and therefore require some other rationale.

Often the report of the dream is erroneous, and on careful inquiry there are symbolic elements that are significantly different from the reality of the dreamer's waking life. The "dream" might also not be truly a dream, for there are levels of consciousness during sleep where dreams more closely resemble waking thoughts. Movement into this kind of "think-ing-dreaming" probably occurs with a shift from REM sleep toward other stages. Some reports of mentation in meditative states characterized by theta waves on the electroence-phalogram resemble such reveries; this may be an explanation for so-called *lucid dreams*, in which the dream-ego presumably knows that it is dreaming and has some control over the content of the dream (a state that I have not, however, seen convincingly demonstrated).

A possible symbolic meaning of a dream that appears to be an exact reproduction of the waking situation is that the un-conscious intends the waking situation to be viewed *as if* it were a dream. The waking situation might itself then be seen in a more symbolic perspective; in terms of compensation, it would mean placing the real situation in a wider context than its everydayness would usually evoke.

Time and Space References

It is unusual for a dream to indicate directly that action takes place in the past or in the future. The dream simply unfolds as if in present time. From the contents of the dream, how-ever, it is generally possible to place it within a particular time frame. A setting or a person from the past included in the present action frequently shows the need to explore a particu-lar segment of the patient's past experience. Conversely, im-ages of the future may be represented by images from another world, another dimension or from an exotic place.

The motif of culturally or technologically advanced persons from outer space may indicate the potential emergence of contents from the unconscious (inner space), and be symbolic of future developments of the dreamer's own ego. (In his doctoral dissertation, Jung noted that the various figures ap-pearing in the mediumistic state might be prefigurations of possible future developments in the personality of the me-dium.)[17]

For example, a man dreamed that what had seemed to be a natural phenomenon in the sky was actually a spaceship, which landed. The dream-ego was part of the greeting delega-tion from earth, walking with the men from space. They walked past a large computer and the dream-ego realized that "our computer was talking to their computer." The entire scene seemed friendly and helpful. In context, this dream suggested that the psychological reorganization taking place did not come from his assimilation of the past but from the inner pressure of future possibilities.

At times, of course, the beings or things from "outer space" may appear maleficent or be more primitive—within the context of the dream—in which case analyst and analysand would be wise to be aware of the potential eruption of archaic impulses.

Synchronistic Phenomena

Synchronicity was the term Jung used to describe the almost simultaneous occurrence in time of two events, one inner and one outer, that seem to have the same meaning.[18] He gave as one example a beetle flying into the room just as he was discussing a patient's recent dream of a scarab. Synchronistic phenomena fall into the same category of events studied by parapsychologists under such names as telepathy, clairvoyance, psychokinesis, etc.

In her collection of spontaneously reported parapsychological or *psi* events, Louise Rhine found that the largest category was associated with dreaming, such as dreams of the future (precognitive dreams) or dreams that contained information not known to the waking-ego (clairvoyant or telepathic dreams).[19] This is certainly consistent with the widespread popular belief that dreams may foretell the future or give information not known to the waking personality of the dreamer. The best experimental evidence for *psi* phenomena in dreams is contained in the laboratory studies reported by Ullman, Krippner and Vaughn in *Dream Telepathy*.[20]

When synchronistic dreams or events occur in psychotherapy they require special awareness and handling, because it is easy for such events to evoke in the patient's mind the idea that the therapist somehow is involved in them (the shamanistic shadow of the analyst). It is also important for the analyst to have some understanding of the possible meanings of synchronistic phenomena. Although many therapists and analysts simply ignore such events as happenstance or chance, they can by very helpful when dealt with seriously.

On a theoretical level, the occurrence of synchronistic dreams are evidence of a close connection between the unconscious of one person and that of another. They may also be taken as evidence that the unconscious is less limited in time and space than the conscious mind. The very occurrence of a synchronistic dream constitutes some compensation by the dream for the limited state of the conscious ego, since the dream shows the dream-ego transcending to some degree the usual constraints of the waking-ego. This is a formal compensation, however, based upon the bare synchronicity; it does not show the meaning of the particular contents of the dream.

Some analysands have frequent dreams that are truly synchronistic. In these cases there is a tendency (by analysand and perhaps also by the analyst) to focus too much upon the synchronicity itself, the formal compensatory aspect of the dream. But, if it is a precognitive dream, for example, one might ask why it is precognitive of one event and not another? The answer to such a question often makes it clear that the synchronistic compensation deals with material that would not necessarily be chosen by the waking-ego if it were offered knowledge of the future.

Synchronistic dreams may occur when there is a need to generate more interest in the analyst or the patient for the process of analysis. In this function, the synchronistic dream is similar in effect to sexualization of the transference-countertransference. It both produces more energy in the analytic situation and calls attention to the mysterious nature of the interaction, which functions at a depth and complexity that is rare in non-analytic relationships.

Early in my psychiatric training, when psychotherapy was to me still a new and exciting skill, there were a number of surprising synchronistic events that caught my attention and caused me to more seriously consider the meaning of such *psi* occurrences. In one instance I was seeing a graduate student in psychology for his third session of therapy. He brought a dream that was long and complicated, but ended with a policeman throwing away an empty cartridge clip and placing a fully loaded magazine in his revolver to continue firing at a thief. At *precisely* the point of this action my ballpoint pen ran out of ink and I excused myself, took another ink cartridge from my desk, refilled the pen and sat down again to write, not realizing the similarity between my action and that in the dream. But the patient noticed! His interest in the analytical process markedly increased on the basis of this strange occurrence, although it was not followed by other such events.

In another instance involving a graduate student early in therapy, the patient never knew of the synchronistic event. I had been trying to remember something my childhood dentist had told me. I could remember everything except the trade name of a product he had described. I could remember only that the active organism was *lactobacillus acidophilus*. On the way to the patient's early morning appointment I was still struggling to recall the trade name. Barely ten sentences into his free associations he began an entirely new line of thought, and suddenly mentioned the name I had been striving for— *lactinex granules*. Although startled, I said nothing to the student because it did not seem to me to be helpful to him—but it had the effect of making me acutely aware of this patient in a way that I had not been previously.

Synchronistic dreams may occur between *any* two persons, having much the same meaning as when they occur in analysis—that is, compensating a too-narrow view of reality, adding attention and energy to the situation, plus whatever specific meaning is carried by the structure and symbolism of the dreams. Sometimes two persons who are intimately involved are in analysis with the same analyst, offering an unusual opportunity to observe parallel dreams, one of the forms in which synchronistic phenomena appear.

In one such case, a man and a woman who had just begun living together reported dreams from the same night with strikingly similar motifs. The woman dreamed that she was with her mother in a large old hotel lobby. The woman who owned the hotel entered with two animals, a German shepherd dog and an oddly colored bear. The bear was not threatening but the dream-ego was afraid. She was torn between making polite conversation with the manager and expressing her fear—a not uncommon feeling in dealings with her mother.

Her boyfriend, meanwhile, had a long and complicated dream which also took place, in part, in a large fancy hotel. In one scene, a man passed by on a motorcycle, with a bear on the seat behind him. The dream-ego wanted to meet the bear, which later seemed to be molesting a dog, but turned out to be quite friendly. He met the trainer of the bear but did not trust him. In other scenes, the dreamer was concerned with various family members, including his ex-wife, whom he found it difficult to stand up to in emotional situations.

These two dreams are abbreviated and it is not the intention here to discuss the rich psychological implications for the two dreamers, but merely to point out the synchronistic parallels: grand hotel, a relative to whom it is difficult to express one's true feelings, dog and bear. This same couple had two other parallel dreams that were less striking because less symbolic. On one occasion, they both dreamed of a mutual friend on the same night; in the other, she dreamed that her ex-husband was in the room with them while he dreamed of seeing the man walking near a synagogue.

It is likely that some synchronistic dreams go unnoticed because they have normal explanations or appear as usual dreams. For example, a woman who felt herself to be particularly open to extrasensory perception was debating whether to go to work in spite of flu symptoms. She thought she was awake when she suddenly experienced in the room the form of a male friend who had died of pulmonary problems. He was dressed as he had usually been in life. He told her she was foolish to go to work with an illness that could kill her, as pneumonia had killed him. On the basis of this "vision" she decided to stay in bed. Was this synchronistic or was it simply a dream or hypnogogic hallucination that dramatized one side of her conflict? There is no way to know. She took it as a visitation from the dead friend's spirit and acted on it as good advice from him. She once needed to talk with her brother about important family matters, but did not know where to reach him since he was on a secret government assignment. Within ten minutes, however, he called her.

In summary, synchronistic dreams and events, if noticed at all, should be dealt with on the same basis as other psychodynamic material, but with particular emphasis on *why* the unconscious used synchronicity to call attention to *what*. One should not "chase" synchronicities or make too much of them, for that can distort the structure of the analysis.

9

Symbolism in Alchemy

Jung was greatly interested in the symbolic content of alchemy, following a series of dreams that led him to investigate the sixteenth-century culture of Europe. He found in alchemical writings a prefiguration of modern depth psychology, although with little differentiation between the literal and the symbolic. The alchemists were attempting the transformation of matter, but did not clearly distinguish their objective work on matter from subjective work on themselves. They therefore tended to project their personal visions of transformation into the mysterious chemical processes they saw taking place in the laboratory.

Some of the later alchemists, however, seemed to be aware that their art was concerned primarily with personal transformation, the search being not for metallic gold but for the inner "gold"; hence they used such terms as "our gold," "the water of the wise," "the diamond body," "treasure hard to attain," etc., to distinguish the inner image from the actual substance. Jung concluded that depth psychology had seemed to have no antecedent only because alchemy had been misunderstood, discarded as simply a footnote in the history of chemistry.

The processes of alchemy are several, although as described in the literature they are by no means standard in number or in sequence, and each has a "penumbra" of lesser images and operations that, when seen in diagrammatic form, look like a complicated road map with various cities surrounded by smaller towns and villages.[21] Among the principle operations, generally speaking, are (in Anglicized form) these seven: solution, coagulation, sublimation, calcination, putrefaction, mortification and conjunction (*coniunctio*).

To each of these chemical operations there are psychological parallels. Calcination, for example, is a chemical method of heating a substance to drive off all moisture and perhaps produce chemical change; psychologically it is related to the drying out of unconscious, "water-logged" complexes. Putting a substance into solution, chemically dissolving it, is analogous to the psychological process of allowing a conscious content to be "dissolved" in the unconscious. The opposite process, coagulation, is chemically like precipitation of a substance from solution and psychologically like the formation of a new complex of ideas from an unconscious matrix. A famous alchemical dictum, "dissolve and coagulate," suggests the repetitive psychological process of realizing that a hard "substance" of the mind—for instance an apparently insoluble conflict—is really capable of solution, only to be replaced by another "substance" that in its turn requires dissolution.

Alchemical Motifs in Dreams

There are dream images and motifs that fall clearly into the range of alchemical symbolism, and it is possible to see alchemical operations behind many others. Dreams where objects of great intrinsic or potential value are treated in a casual way, for instance, suggest the alchemical image of the *prima materia*—that base and apparently worthless substance from which, through the alchemical operations, one can produce what is of highest value, called variously the philosopher's stone, elixir of the wise, aqua vitae, the panacea, etc. Dream images of minted gold coins found mixed in among the pebbles of a stream, or strewn unnoticed in the dust of a supermarket parking lot are examples of *prima materia* imagery.

The process of *calcinatio* can be shown by figures existing unharmed in a fire; the figures may be human or animal, in rare instances with the appearance of the fire-dwelling salamander (another alchemical image of the *prima materia*). When figures accept their presence in a fire (in one dream, playing cards amid the flames) it suggests that transformation by fire (emotional heat) is necessary, however inappropriate it may seem from the view of the dream-ego—or however painful it is to the waking-ego. Consider one man's dream:

> A large frog was in the fire. It resembled Yoda in the *Star Wars* movie. I was amazed that it remained alive so long in the fire. It looked at me. Finally it shrunk and was black. In the next scene (maybe a second dream of the same night) it is as if I am looking through the eyes of an aborigine who holds a

steel grill over an open fire. On the grill are a miniature tiger and a kangaroo that are fighting each other and also trying to get off the grill. The aborigine flicks them back on the grill. Finally, like the frog, they are shrunken and charred.

The dreamer's associations were few: he considered the kangaroo maternal and shy and was surprised that it was not afraid of the tiger. The dream shows the frog-like creature acquiescing in a *calcinatio* experience, leading to two warring opposites that must be held in that tension by a primitive ego structure (the aborigine). The transformation of the tiger and the kangaroo into "higher" substances is not shown in this dream, but in a later dream of the same man a more human preparation for change was indicated, involving the imagery of *mortificatio* (dying):

I was looking over a possible construction site. There were bulldozers clearing it. One large building seemed to be deserted and would be torn down. I went into the building. It did seem deserted, but when I got to the very back of the structure I found an old priest who was taking care of a number of terminal patients, all of whom would die. He was making sure that they died in a dignified way. I was going to see that the building was left undisturbed until they were all gone. Then I was in a helicopter flying over the site looking at plans for the new construction. I could see the entire area from the air.

On the basis of this dream he took a brief leave of absence from analysis, which seemed a responsible decision.

Coffee turning into golden liquid as it circulates through a percolator suggests the alchemical motif of *circulatio,* a continual recycling of the *prima materia.* Alchemical operations pictured in dreams often take place in a kitchen, a setting similar to the alchemical laboratory.

Coniunctio: Images of Union

Alchemical imagery shows various operations that lead up to the *coniunctio,* the union of the opposites; hence *coniunctio* imagery in dreams seems clinically to be more closely related to the final goal of alchemical processes than are the other operations.

In the alchemical illustrations to "The Psychology of the

Transference," Jung chose images that emphasize the human-like quality of the *coniunctio:* a king and a queen are literally joined into one person following sexual union, but that joined entity is dead and must be resurrected by the return of the soul. Sexual images in dreams frequently fit into this alchemical operation of *coniunctio,* particularly when they are incestuous or with an unknown dream figure. There can, of course, be frankly sexual dreams that are simply compensatory to sexual frustration in waking life; the context will tell.

A more subtle form of the *coniunctio* imagery is the wedding motif. The dream-ego may be simply an observer at the wedding, not a principal, showing that the opposites to be united are outside the dream-ego (though perhaps within the structure of the waking-ego). Indeed, in most instances it is not the dream-ego that undergoes what has been compared to the alchemical processes; rather it is the *prima materia,* the unvalued substance of ordinary psychic life, or the everydayness of actual outer life, that is transformed. In one case, the dream-ego of a woman was simply assisting a bride to dress for her wedding. The only unusual image was the crown of the bride, which was cubical in form, open in front and back and covered with satin. In another instance, the dream-ego simply drove two women to a wedding at which they were to be guests, while a major transformation occurred in imagery that had frightened the dream-ego earlier in the dream.

The sexual mating of animals in dreams sometimes produces not offspring but changes in the mating figures themselves—not a "natural" image, but one that points to the transformation within the dreamer of an instinctual conflict.

Observing the appearance of *coniunctio* imagery in a dream series can give clues as to when the reconciliation of a particular pair of warring opposites may be expected. Sometimes this is reflected in the easing of a conscious conflict; at other times the result on the level of conscious life may be no more than a lessening of depression or anxiety. Much of the work of analysis, indeed, seems to be to maintain a steady and reliable containing structure in which preparations for the *coniunctio* can safely take place.

Dreams that do not correspond naturally with the imagery of alchemy should not be forced to fit, nor should motifs that are not clearly evident be overinterpreted. (The danger of archetypal reductionism lurks constantly in the Jungian consulting room.) There are always more dreams than are remembered or brought for analysis, and these too can be quietly working for change. We must never forget that analysts are for the most part midwives and facilitators — the onlookers at a mysterious process, not the originators of the process.

10

Dreams and Individuation

The Nature of Neurosis

The most commonsense description of neurosis is this: the psyche working against itself, like a country in civil war, rather than as a unified whole. To some extent we are all neurotic, in the sense that we seldom are "at one" with ourselves. The mere existence of parts of the psyche, such as ego and shadow, implies that they will not necessarily work in unison. But excessive incongruence or conflict between the dominant ego-image and other active parts of the psyche is characteristic of chronic neurosis, one of the most difficult of human conditions to alter.

Dreams are compensatory in all states of psychological functioning—in ordinary life (where they compensate the individuation process), in psychosis (where they attempt to produce a stable ego), and in neurosis, where they are active in bringing the ego out of a neurotic byway or impasse and into the mainstream of individuation. Individuation takes place in any state of the psyche, whether a person is conscious or unconscious, but it is most facilitated when the ego consciously and intentionally observes the movements of the psyche, takes an attitude toward them and responsibly participates in the evolution of the psyche as a whole.

No true life task can be avoided, it can only be approached in an oblique or substitute way. The symptoms of neurosis are often substitutes for the more direct life experience that is shunned out of fear. A lack of normal assertiveness may result in neurotic symptoms of chronic anxiety, so that situations normally not fearful come to evoke fear—as if the psyche produces a superabundance of situations in which the needed development might take place. A person seeking to motivate himself by self-suggestion rather than characterological growth may find the suggestions failing and depression arising. If introversion is needed yet avoided, psychosomatic symptoms may force a period of introversion. These movements of the psyche are subtle but they are not weak.

Neurotics are characterized by an adaptation to the world

101

that appears quite normal when viewed from outside. They usually accomplish the basic life tasks well enough, but at the expense of excessive internal stress. In one sense, it requires a more developed psychic structure to become neurotic rather than simply suffer conflict with others in the environment. The neurotic is able to internalize conflict, setting up complex intrapsychic structures that insulate the ego from the original conflict but produce substitute conflicts which appear less meaningful until observed analytically.

The neurotic ego is already by and large stable and well enough formed, although identified with ego-images that shield it from direct involvement in further individuation. This is sometimes in the service of maintaining a stage of the past that was particularly enjoyable, so that the ego is partially fixated through a clinging to the pleasures of the past state. Fixation may also occur because of a severe trauma in the past, the ego trying either to reproduce the traumatic situation so that it can be solved or to compensate in the present for the trauma of the past: in either case the present is sacrificed to a dynamic relationship to the past. If these choices were clearly conscious there would be no problem. The individual could simply recognize the mistake and abandon the neurotic task or accept a particular form of the task and devote oneself to potential solutions. Since the choices are unconscious, however, what the ego experiences is a curious and perverse repetition of events; at a deeper level, the choice is made by the ego itself, but dissociated from the current dominant ego-image.

Throughout life the Self exerts a continuous pressure on the ego both to face reality and to participate in the process of individuation. It does this with or without the ego's willing consent, but the compensations against a reluctant ego (nightmares, accidents, physical symptoms, etc.) are usually more severe than the complementary relationship of the unconscious to an ego that is doing its best to participate consciously in the individuation process.

How can dreams help?

An understanding of dreams reveals recurrent patterns to the ego, patterns in which it is often possible to discover repetitive mistakes presented in different ways. When these conflicts are clearly seen there is a possibility for more direct action in a responsible direction. Dreams are in the service of the psyche as a whole and are only secondarily opposed to any particular attitude or standpoint of the ego. By seeing what the dreams are already trying to accomplish, the waking-ego is able to assess its own position and participate, if it wills to, in the deeper processes. It is *not* that the waking-ego can simply turn the course of its life over to dreams as if to guides (a common misunderstanding). It is absolutely necessary for the waking-ego to know its own position in order for the dreams to have a clear compensatory role, their natural function in the healthy psyche.

Dreams that show the ego forced to deal with threatening situations are particularly indicative of neurotically delayed development. Dreams of threatening figures that become less so as they approach the dream-ego, for instance, point up the excessive fear of facing unintegrated contents of the psyche. It is in this stage of ego growth that archetypal imagery of the heroic struggle or quest is particularly applicable, for the immature ego rarely achieves a mature state without facing fearful and potentially threatening situations. There are many parallels in mythology and folklore for these developments. Fairytales in particular seem to be a rich depository of modes of ego development and may be used to advantage in amplifying dreams that deal with this struggle. Fairytales also point to the multiplicity of forms of ego development in both men and women. There is usually a fearful and regressive force to be overcome (such as a dragon) or a hostile or indolent parental image (the old king or the jealous stepmother queen, etc). In addition there are helpers, often talking animals that know more of the natural wisdom of life than the ego possesses. The dream motif of a helpful animal capable of speech may indicate that the unconscious is ready to help the ego in its task; such dreams seem particularly good prognostic signs.

The very multiplicity of fairytale motifs reminds us that there are many different ways for the immature ego to develop. Not all are heroic struggles; occasionally there is a fairytale that shows the ego unable to accomplish anything on its own, so that it must wait for rescue from outside. Clinically this would involve a much more active and supporting role for the analyst or the therapy group; more containing and nurturing would be necessary before the ego of the analysand could be expected to make the first independent movements on its own behalf.

In one case, a woman who had lived her life contained in traditional feminine roles had a brief, unhappy and inappropriate relationship with a man much younger than herself, leading to depression and then to psychotherapy. As she began to improve she dreamed of a strange flower that was also an animal; and it was somehow both male and female at one time. This motif indicated the unification of opposites (plant/animal, male/female) suggestive of the Self. She painted the dream, and from that point onward began the development of a more independent personality.

In another instance, a woman beginning to assert herself dreamed that she was in a large room in the presence of another woman with a similar problem. A man who had carried in projected form much of her latent potential was sitting at a desk working. His wife approached in an angry jealous rage and verbally criticized the dream-ego in a scathing manner. The dream-ego saw a "red king" to the left of the scene of confrontation and threw over the king a cloak embroidered with four rabbits. She herself was somehow the cloak. The dream suggests that her own independence (the king) is still hidden with a cloak of rabbit qualities—perhaps the old, not quite discarded rabbit-like timidity.

In a third case, a man dreams that his guard dog, actually deceased, is alive and speaks to him, asking to be taken into the house rather than being left in the yard. This dream indicates an appropriately aggressive guarding function wishing to be more integrated. The speaking animal shows that content to be near the point of ego integration; the qualities of the dog had previously appeared only in regressive and destructive form, erupting at unexpected times.

The Relativization of the Ego

The movement out of neurosis also involves the relativization of a strong ego. The developed ego is asked to confront again the unconscious matrix from which it has freed itself in the first stages of the individuation process. Teleologically speaking, it is as if the purpose of the overall process of individuation were for the unconscious to become known and recognized as the source. The ego, after all, is a specialized outgrowth of the unconscious, its position as the center of the conscious field being analogous to its archetypal template, the Self, as the center of the psyche as a whole. Dream imagery pointing to the need for this realization is less likely to picture heroic tasks of confrontation, but may show the nature of reality in a surprising manner—including symbols of the Self that do not seem to be compensating a weak ego structure but exist in their own right, without a strong dynamic relationship to the current neurotic conflicts. Amplifications at this stage may more appropriately be found in religious traditions than in fairytales, although all "rules" must be held lightly in this regard for there is no clear division between stages of individuation; moreover, when we speak of a pattern we speak of a generality, while the process in any actual person is always unique and more problematic.

A person dreams of a mandala-like city, for example, which it is possible to enter or not as the ego chooses. A variant of that theme is a building of immense size, often symmetrical in shape. There may be insights into the living nature of the world, as in a dream of seeing a large matrix of one animal with many heads that lives simply on air; its size is awesome but its nature is gentle and non-threatening.

The relativization of the ego may also involve impressive dreams in which no ego action is necessary, in contrast to the heroic activity often required of the dream-ego in earlier stages of differentiation. Initiation images may appear, indicating that the ego is to enter another stage of activity. Dream motifs of "letting go," referring to problems that have not been solved, particularly tend to occur when the time available for individuation is being cut short, as in terminal illness.

The Individuating Ego

Jungian psychology appreciates with unusual clarity the relative nature of the ego.[22] In most psychotherapeutic systems, the development of a strong and independent ego is the major emphasis, although tempered with the need to achieve close, loving relationships. Jungian psychology also values these aims, but the vision of individuation as a basic life process prevents their becoming overemphasized. Any state of ego-identity is seen as relative to the person's own individuation process, no matter how successful one may be in terms of adaptation to the environment or to others.

The natural inclination of the ego is to see itself as the center of the psyche, although it is only the center of the virtual conscious world, in itself always a particular construction from the many archetypal possibilities. The ego is like the hereditary monarch of a country who is the only available ruler, but who cannot control everything that happens within his domain nor be completely conscious of all that happens or might happen.

The goal of Jungian analysis is not simply the therapeutic construction of an adequately functioning ego—although many analysands choose to stop then, for at that point one feels major relief from the neurotic unhappiness that leads most persons into therapy or analysis. But if work with the unconscious is carried beyond the alleviation of neurotic suffering, it leads imperceptibly into the consideration of philosophical, religious and ethical issues on a level very different from their consideration on a simply collective conscious basis. Questions that for a merely strong ego would be a simple matter of decision may become for the individuating ego serious ethical concerns, for nothing is outside the process of individuation and there is no clear, ready-made framework for decisions. In making choices one is always also choosing one self from among the several "selves" that might be actualized.

Whether to take one job or another, for example, might be a matter of conscious preference. But the individuating ego is making a more momentous decision. Dreams may show this, as in the dream of a man who considered a job that would take him away from dealing with people and allow him to maintain his neurotic isolation. After deciding in favor of such an "evasive" job, he dreamed that he was attracted to a woman he knew to be dead and was prevented from following her onto a ship (ship of death?) only by the action of another figure outside the dream-ego. Similarly, recurrent dreams of persistent knocking at the door may symbolize contents that have been left out of the dreamer's life and are insisting on being heard, although one does not know at that point what they actually are.

The relative nature of the ego can be seen over time but it can also be appreciated in the fine structure of the relationship of the dream-ego to the waking-ego. The archetypal core of the ego, the Self, has a centering quality, although it also breaks up incomplete formations in order to bring them into a more inclusive structure. This archetypal background underlies the sense of "I" the ego has as the center of subjectivity. Other complexes act as partial personalities, and even have wills of their own independent of the ego, as can be seen in many situations. But until a content experiences a connection with the ego it does not participate in the sense of "I." This is most evident in the relations of the ego with the identity structures of persona and shadow. Until it is integrated into the ego, the persona feels like a role that one can play or not play. But new ego contents may enter via the route of a persona role, later becoming part of the ego structure itself. Similarly, the shadow classically appears in non-ego projection onto someone in the environment; later it must be painfully reabsorbed and experienced as a potential part of "I."

Dreams offer the most microscopic field to observe the fine structure of the ego complex. In the day-to-day compensations of dreams one sees the same interaction of ego and the Self (as dream maker) that can be seen in macroscopic vision over the decades and stages of life. In addition to its clinical usefulness, such observation of the relativity of the ego in dreams and waking life can lead to an appreciation of the care and rectitude with which dreams compensate the waking-ego. It is much like having a wise but impartial friend, who knows things about oneself that one may suspect but does not yet know in full consciousness.

The Dream-Ego and the Waking-Ego

The structural relationship between the dream-ego and the waking-ego can be pictured as similar to that which prevails within a government. The ego is the only possible ruler but can be swayed by the acts of other forces that are necessary to the government as a whole. The waking-ego is the responsible representative for all that is done in the name of the individual psyche, and is even held legally accountable in society. But in the dream state the waking-ego is not present in its complexity and multileveled reality. Instead, the dream-ego finds itself with the same responsibilities as the waking-ego but in a dream world that is not of its choosing. In the dream world (as in the waking world) persons and situations arise that are not to the liking of the ego; the tasks of the dream are not chosen but are *given,* just as the everyday world has an objective reality outside the ego.

The situation of the dream-ego may be taken as analogous to a committee structure in the government of the waking-ego. The waking-ego is the president or king, while the dream-ego is chairperson of a *part* of the structure that participates in the waking-ego's world. The "committee," however is not illusory, not "just a dream." It is a part, albeit only a part, of the entire waking-ego structure, hence the actions (or lack of them) of the dream-ego can affect the world of the waking-ego. Actions that result in structural changes in the world of the dream-ego may be inherited in several ways by the waking-ego in its world. The most usual way of experiencing such changes are alterations in the emotional states of the waking-ego: a lightening of depression, a decrease or increase in anxiety, a sense of "the right decision" in a problematic situation, etc.

This dialogue between the waking-ego and the dream, mediated by the dream-ego, is part of the larger dialogue between the ego and the Self. The Self is not often imaged in a dream, at least not recognizably. It is more often evident as the unseen constructor of the dream, that force in the psyche which not only arranges the scenes and the action but also assigns the dream-ego to a particular role. This does not mean, however, that the dream is entirely formed before it is experienced by the dreamer, for the actions of the dream-ego seem to be crucial in what follows after such action. (Even in the repetitive dreams characteristic of traumatic neurosis, it is potentially more therapeutic to see the dream-ego as trying, however unsuccessfully, to initiate a change.)

The individuating ego inevitably realizes that *neither* the dream-ego nor the waking-ego is *the* ego. The ego centrum, the sense of "I," is merely the current, subjective point of reference for the process of individuation, which relativizes the waking-ego over time in a manner similar to the smaller relativizations that occur nightly in the experience of the dream-ego.

These insights have practical implications in dream interpretation. The relativity of the ego argues against taking any ego-state as fixed, so that it is not appropriate to speak of right choices or wrong choices by the waking-ego. Except within very broad legal and ethical boundaries, the waking-ego's choices simply influence its own constellation of its own world, which is not "right or wrong" but "preferred or not preferred," or "authentic or inauthentic." The relativity of the ego in relation to the other structures of the psyche, such as shadow and persona, also lends an appreciation of how the waking-ego can be influenced through the action of parts of the psyche of which it is unaware. For instance, the ego may quite unnecessarily hide its reality behind a transient use of the persona—not a pathological identification with the persona, but an autonomous manifestation of *its* will; and unconscious aspects of the shadow can lead the waking-ego to actions and attitudes that the ego itself would deem unworthy if they were clearly presented for judgment.

Working with dreams as a part of the analytical situation gives the waking-ego a sense of its own relativity in relation to the dream-ego. Dreams of shadow experiences (of a positive or negative nature), as well as dramatic presentations of ways in which the waking-ego functions, can lead to a very valuable awareness by the waking-ego of its own vulnerability. Armed with this awareness, the waking-ego is more easily able to recognize inflation, avoid identification with other parts of the psyche, and minimize the consequences of projection through memories of how strong emotional reactions to others in the past eventually "came home to roost" as aspects of one's own shadow or anima/animus.

Focal and Tacit Knowing

Although good clinical work can be done with a minimum of theoretical understanding, it is useful to have at least a skeletal theoretical structure in order to orient oneself in the shifting directions of the clinical situation. One way to conceptualize the relativity of the ego is in terms of *focal* and *tacit knowing*, terms derived from the epistemological work of Michael Polanyi.[23]

Polanyi speaks of the structure of *all* knowledge as having a "from-to" nature. We rely upon knowing some contents tacitly in order to know other contents in a more focal manner. The microscope, for instance, is a tacit structure (as is the eye) for focal knowledge of microorganisms or other objects. Polanyi's conclusions emphasize that there is an irreducible element of personal commitment and risk in trying to be objective about anything at all. We make factual statements with universal intent, confident that any unbiased observer will come to the same conclusion, but we know that we cannot help our personal involvement, which determines to some degree not only what we see but what we choose to be worthy of observation in the first place.

The compartments of focal and tacit knowledge are the universal structure of knowing, Polanyi asserts, but their contents may shift. What is tacit at one point may be focal at another. The tacit compartment of knowledge is similar to the *unconscious* but not exactly equivalent, for one can consciously choose to use something in a tacit manner, as when speech is considered tacit in relation to the *meaning* to which it points. Similarly, focal knowledge is analogous to the field of consciousness; it may be *pre*conscious but in general is easily brought into the light of conscious awareness.

Applying these concepts to the dream-ego and the waking-ego, one could say that the waking-ego relies in a tacit manner upon contents of the psyche that would appear to the dream-ego as focal. A complex that acts as part of the background awareness of the waking-ego (therefore as a part of the tacit structure of the waking-ego) can be personified by a dream figure in relation to the dream-ego. The action of the dream-ego with that figure would then potentially alter the tacit structure upon which the waking-ego will rely, after the dream, for its own sense of tacit awareness of the world. The activity of the dream-ego is thus conceptualized as an extension into the dream world of the same process of individuation that is the deeper task of the waking-ego. The dream is seen as a symbolic structure that presents the dream-ego with chosen aspects of the structure of the waking-ego. The relation of the dream-ego and the waking-ego is then seen as a profoundly helpful interplay between the focal and tacit compartments of ego-identity.

The analyst is in a unique position not only to observe such focal/tacit changes between the dream-ego and the waking-ego, but also to facilitate the analysand's awareness of this process. Indeed, when one is sufficiently aware of these relationships, and has some skill in dealing with dreams, the necessity of formal analytical sessions begins to diminish. Although formal analysis always ends at some point in time, the process of analytical awareness continues throughout life. At times a resumption of formal analysis is indicated or desired, but the developed or differentiated ego, aware of its relativity, can make good use of many dreams without having to discuss them in an analytical relationship.

11

The Two Tensions of Dream Interpretation

Two tensions are continually present in the successful use of dream interpretation. The first is the tension between objective and subjective interpretations of dream motifs. The second is characteristic not only of dream interpretation but of the entire analytic process; it is the tension between the personal and archetypal meanings.

Objective and Subjective

In suggesting that the images and motifs in a dream could be considered either objectively (referring to persons or events in waking life) or subjectively (as an aspect of the dreamer's own psyche) Jung expressed in practical clinical form a tension that has been inherent in the study of dreams since antiquity. Freud reduced this tension by postulating that dreams were simply former waking thoughts and wishes that were unacceptable to the ego; if the "latent" dream behind the experienced "manifest" dream were brought into full consciousness it would only be a former waking thought that had been repressed.

The tension between the objective and the subjective meaning of dreams can also be reduced, perhaps too easily, by considering that dreams *always* refer to subjective representation in the mind of the dreamer. Some of these subjective meanings are object representations, in the mind, of real external persons and situations. In this view dreams are seen as changing only the internal representation of things, which of course affects the external experience, because the waking-ego relies upon such object representations in a tacit manner for its own sense of orientation in waking reality.

The tension between the objective and the subjective, however, is more profound. There is little danger in a non-psychotic state of seeing some dreams in terms of outer reality alone, and the limitation to only subjective meanings would rob us of a tension that is psychologically fruitful.

Waking and dreaming experiences are not in primal opposition. There is no mysterious dream world that is in stark contrast to an entirely objective "dayworld." *Both* waking conscious experience and experiences in dreams are equally mysterious components of a potential unity—the process of individuation. Dreams pass quickly away, but also (although more slowly) do the "firm" realities of waking life. Amid the flux of change there can appear the very mysterious process that Jung called individuation, involving the actualization of one's unique potentials to whatever extent and in whatever manner is permitted by the vicissitudes of life.

In waking, "objective" existence the movement of individuation is not always in terms of what is "logical" to do, just as in fairytales it is often not the older, more mature prince who rescues the endangered princess—it may be his younger, stumbling, bumbling brother who uses unorthodox methods such as helpful animals. In any series of dreams the movement may be *into* objective life situations or *away* from them. There is no set rule. In the service of individuation, dreams may impel the ego toward establishing itself in ordinary cultural identities. At other times, the dreams may pull the ego straight out of its successful waking adaptation and face it with more subtle meanings and tasks.

The final resolution of the tension between the objective and the subjective is a sense of what Jung described as the circumambulation of a mysterious center of the psyche, which can be felt but never defined in the nets of consciousness. In this mysterious process, psychologically analogous to the alchemical quest, the ego is relativized but not soft, events are real but not overwhelming, images in dreams are guides but not masters. The process of individuation is what is finally served and facilitated by dreams, although dreams can be used *along the way* in the ordinary psychotherapeutic tasks of problem solving and personality development.

The Personal and the Archetypal

Another way of stating the tension involved in psychological individuation is in terms of the opposition of personal and archetypal. When a person is too deeply embedded in the collective, outer reality of everyday life, the discovery in his or her own dreams of universal, archetypal images from the objective depths of the psyche can be a freeing experience. But if one is ordinarily prey to a rampant, schizophrenic confusion of archetypal images, the achievement of a stable ego standpoint is equally experienced as liberation.

Both the neurotic caught in excessive concretization of family or social "realities" and the schizophrenic drowning in a sea of archetypal meanings find a sense of haven in what might be called the personal sphere of life. Personal history is one's own deeper sense of meaning and continuity, not simply the pseudopersonal history of dates and outer events, the usual clothesline of life on which various roles are hung as old garments. External life may go through profound changes without any alteration in the subjective perception of the meaning of life. But every therapist knows of the opposite situation in which outer life goes along smooth and unchanging while the inner subjective state is transformed into what is essentially an entirely new and fresh world of meaning.

The waking-ego exists between two equally dangerous archetypal constellations. We are accustomed in Jungian psychology to think of the archetypal realm of the collective unconscious, the objective psyche, as a counterpoint to the rigid constructions of the waking-ego. We are less accustomed to think of the archetypal origins of the world of collective consciousness. Yet both these worlds that surround the ego on its inner and outer frontiers are archetypal.

The world of collective consciousness (history as we read it) is shaped by certain individuals expressing archetypal contents that arise from the objective psyche. Many do this and fail to have a cultural impact, but others strike a particularly ready response in their culture or society and alter it to a greater or lesser extent. Archetypal forms that are enshrined in cultural institutions become the tacit furniture of the collective conscious mind. But the moment an archetypal form is embedded in a cultural institution, the institution is in opposition to the very archetype that gave it birth, for no one particular form can carry the full range of meaning of an archetypal possibility.

What is true on a societal level is also true of the individual psyche. No real personal mother can embody all the range of possibilities inherent in the archetypal Great Mother, so that the mother imago in the mind is both a carrier and a restriction of the mother archetype. The same is true of all archetypal forms, including Jung's visionary image of God defecating on Basel Cathedral.[24]

The individual ego can lose its way in either the archetypal images of the collective unconscious—particularly when they are used as an escape from tasks in outer life—or in the archetypal forms embedded in the institutions of collective consciousness and culture. The problem is to find a personal standpoint that can relativize these archetypal realms—not placing them in opposition, not identifying one as true and the other false, and without losing the personal sphere, the only space in which the deep transforming processes can occur.

Nothing of *psychological* importance occurs outside the personal sphere. There may be great sound and fury, and enormous sweeps of historical change, but the individual psyche is the only carrier (and ultimately the transmitter) for the archetypal forms that are attempting to reach a stable organic equilibrium. Hence maintenance of the personal sphere is of the utmost importance, both in analysis and in everyday life.

Disruption of the personal sphere occurs in analysis when the archetypal realm is overemphasized, often signalled by an archetypally distorted transference—the analyst being seen as too god-like or too devil-like. In either case, there ceases to be a human interaction. Or the analysand may devalue the analytical process itself and seek refuge in a culturally embedded archetypal form, such as a political party or an organized religion. Such developments are tragic, for the transformative field of the analytic interaction is a rare and valuable place; for some it is the only hope of ever finding a truly personal sphere, and the only opportunity for conscious, non-neurotic participation in their own process of individuation.

When used with care and clinical skill, dreams are the most appropriate and reliable guide to maintaining the personal sphere and avoiding the two forms of archetypal reductionism.

A Brief Summing-Up

Dreams are a natural part of the life of the psyche. They serve the individuation process through compensating distorted models of reality held by the waking-ego.

The dream must be recorded as nearly as possible as it actually occurred. Interpolations from the waking-ego should be resisted. Even dreams that approximate waking reality often have a symbolic nuance.

In amplifying dream motifs, personal associations should usually take precedence over cultural or archetypal amplifications, although some dreams can be understood only in the light of transpersonal material. The amplified dream must be firmly placed in the context of the dreamer's life.

Dreams can be a valuable aid in such clinical concerns as differential diagnosis, assessment of prognosis, and in making decisions about additional supports such as medication, frequency of analytic hours and hospitalization. Dreams are also guides to when to emphasize reductive or prospective modes of analysis.

A series of dreams offers corrections to mistaken interpretations of a particular dream. Exact motifs seldom recur; more frequently there seem to be related images that cluster about the same complexes. Following images and motifs in a series of dreams can give the analyst and analysand a special understanding of the underlying individuation process that dreams are trying to further.

Dreams are particularly useful in the treatment of neurosis. Neurotic conflicts are often symptomatic of the avoidance of appropriate life tasks. In neurosis the dreams are already attempting to overcome the neurotic split, encouraging the ego to deal with actual life processes rather than neurotic substitutes. In the treatment of neurosis the ego is brought back to face the basic movement of individuation, which involves both the development of a strong ego and the realization by the ego of its partial nature in comparison to the more complete wholeness represented by the Self.

Dreams must not be overused or allowed to seduce the analytical process away from other material that obviously

116

needs attention. When there are no dreams, analysis can proceed with whatever is at hand—the transference-countertransference, review of the past, the events of daily life, occurrences in group therapy, sandtray projections, etc. Dreams serve the process, but are not themselves the process of individuation.

Responsible dream analysis preserves the tension between objective and subjective meanings as well as the broader tensions between the personal sphere and the archetypal forces that surround it.

*

A dream is a piece of reality whose origin is personal but obscure, whose meaning is pregnant but uncertain and whose fate in the world of the waking-ego lies in our own hands. If we treat it with respect and concern, it serves us in many ways. If we disregard the dream, it moves us in any case, working its alchemical transformations in the depths of the psyche, seeking the same goal of individuation with or without our conscious aid.

Dreams are mysterious entities, like messages from an unknown friend who is caring but objective. The handwriting and the language are at times obscure, but there is never any doubt as to the underlying concern for our ultimate welfare—which may be different from the state of well-being that we imagine to be our goal.

Humility is necessary. No dream is ever fully understood; future events and future dreams may modify what seemed to be a perfectly complete interpretation. We must always be aware of the mysterious nature of dreams, which exist at the border of our understanding of brain and mind, conscious and unconscious, personal and transpersonal life.

Notes

CW—*The Collected Works of C.G. Jung* (Bollingen Series XX). 20 vols. Trans. R.F.C. Hull. Ed. H. Read, M. Fordham, G. Adler, Wm. McGuire. Princeton University Press, Princeton, 1953-1979.

1. See "Wotan," and "After the Catastrophe," in *Civilization in Transition,* CW 10.
2. See Jolande Jacobi, *The Way of Individuation,* trans. R.F.C. Hull (London: Hodder and Stoughton, 1967).
3. See H.P. Roffwarg, W.C. Dement, J.N. Muzio et al, "Dream Imagery: Relationship to Rapid Eye Movements of Sleep," *Archives of General Psychiatry* 7 (1962): 235-258.
4. See James A. Hall, *Clinical Uses of Dreams: Jungian Interpretations and Enactments* (New York: Grune and Stratton, 1977), pp. 163-179; and M. Polanyi, *Personal Knowledge: Toward a Post-Critical Philosophy* (Chicago: University of Chicago Press, 1958).
5. *Redemption Motifs in Fairytales* (Toronto: Inner City Books, 1980), pp. 17-18.
6. Hall, *Clinical Uses of Dreams,* pp. 151-161.
7. Ibid., pp. 331-347.
8. *Face to Face,* BBC Production, 1961.
9. "The Psychology of the Transference," in *The Practice of Psychotherapy,* CW 16. The other major source of Jung's thoughts on transference and countertransference is "The Tavistock Lectures" (particularly Lecture V), in *The Symbolic Life,* CW 20.
10. Ibid., pars. 334-336.
11. Ibid., par. 331.
12. *Experimental Researches,* CW 2, pars. 733, 1351.
13. See "The Psychology of Dementia Praecox," in *The Psychogenesis of Mental Disease,* CW 3, par. 86. I have slightly expanded the concept of the affect-ego in relating it to object relations theory (see my *Clinical Uses of Dreams,* pp. 49-52).
14. *Memories, Dreams, Reflections,* trans. Richard and Clara Winston, ed. Aniela Jaffé (London: Collins Fontana Library, 1967), pp. 354-355.
15. Hall, *Clinical Uses of Dreams,* pp. 269-271.

16. Some of the motifs presented here, and many others, are discussed at more length in my *Clinical Uses of Dreams*, pp. 275-327.

17. "On the Psychology and Pathology of So-Called Occult Phenomena," in *Psychiatric Studies*, CW 1. For Jung's later views on the psychological significance of "outer space" phenomena, both in waking life and in dreams, see "Flying Saucers: A Modern Myth," in *Civilization in Transition*, CW 10.

18. See "Synchronicity: An Acausal Connecting Principle," in *The Structure and Dynamics of the Psyche*, CW 8.

19. See Louise Rhine, *Hidden Channels of the Mind* (New York: Sloan, 1961), and "Psychological Processes in ESP Experiences: I. Waking Experiences; II. Dreams," *Journal of Parapsychology* 26 (1962): 88-111, 171-199.

20. M. Ullman, S. Krippner and A. Vaughn, *Dream Telepathy* (New York: Macmillan, 1973). See also M. Ullman, "An Experimental Approach to Dreams and Telepathy," in *Archives of General Psychiatry* 14 (1966): 605-613.

21. An excellent presentation of alchemical procedures and their psychological analogies appears in Edward Edinger's articles, "Psychotherapy and Alchemy," in *Quadrant* (Journal of the New York C.G. Jung Foundation), 11-15 (Spring 1978 to Spring 1982). Another useful study of alchemical symbolism and the psychological implications is Marie-Louise von Franz, *Alchemy: An Introduction to the Symbolism and the Psychology* (Toronto: Inner City Books, 1980).

    With regard to *coniunctio* imagery, see my essay "Enantiodromia and the Unification of Opposites," in *The Arms of the Windmill: Essays in Analytical Psychology in Honor of Werner H. Engel*, ed. Joan Carson (New York: privately printed, 1983).

22. Hall, *Clinical Uses of Dreams*, pp. 146-150.

23. Polanyi, *Personal Knowledge*.

24. *Memories, Dreams, Reflections*, p. 56.

Glossary of Jungian Terms

Anima (Latin, "soul"). The unconscious, feminine side of a man's personality. She is personified in dreams by images of women ranging from prostitute and seductress to spiritual guide (Wisdom). She is the eros principle, hence a man's anima development is reflected in how he relates to women. Identification with the anima can appear as moodiness, effeminacy, and oversensitivity. Jung calls the anima *the archetype of life itself.*

Animus (Latin, "spirit"). The unconscious, masculine side of a woman's personality. He personifies the logos principle. Identification with the animus can cause a woman to become rigid, opinionated, and argumentative. More positively, he is the inner man who acts as a bridge between the woman's ego and her own creative resources in the unconscious.

Archetypes. Irrepresentable in themselves, but their effects appear in consciousness as the archetypal images and ideas. These are universal patterns or motifs which come from the collective unconscious and are the basic content of religions, mythologies, legends, and fairytales. They emerge in individuals through dreams and visions.

Association. A spontaneous flow of interconnected thoughts and images around a specific idea, determined by unconscious connections.

Complex. An emotionally charged group of ideas or images. At the "center" of a complex is an archetype or archetypal image.

Constellate. Whenever there is a strong emotional reaction to a person or a situation, a complex has been constellated (activated).

Ego. The central complex in the field of consciousness. A strong ego can relate objectively to activated contents of the unconscious (i.e., other complexes), rather than identifying with them, which appears as a state of possession.

Feeling. One of the four psychic functions. It is a rational function which evaluates the worth of relationships and situations. Feeling must be distinguished from emotion, which is due to an activated complex.

Individuation. The conscious realization of one's unique psychological reality, including both strengths and limitations. It leads to the experience of the Self as the regulating center of the psyche.

Inflation. A state in which one has an unrealistically high or low (negative inflation) sense of identity. It indicates a regression of consciousness into unconsciousness, which typically happens when the ego takes too many unconscious contents upon itself and loses the faculty of discrimination.

Intuition. One of the four psychic functions. It is the irrational function which tells us the possibilities inherent in the present. In contrast to sensation (the function which perceives immediate reality through the physical senses) intuition perceives via the unconscious, e.g., flashes of insight of unknown origin.

120

Participation mystique. A term derived from the anthropologist Lévy-Bruhl, denoting a primitive, psychological connection with objects, or between persons, resulting in a strong unconscious bond.

Persona (Latin, "actor's mask"). One's social role, derived from the expectations of society and early training. A strong ego relates to the outside world through a flexible persona; identification with a specific persona (doctor, scholar, artist, etc.) inhibits psych. logical development.

Projection. The process whereby an unconscious quality or characteristic of one's own is perceived and reacted to in an outer object or person. Projection of the anima or animus onto a real women or man is experienced as falling in love. Frustrated expectations indicate the need to withdraw projections, in order to relate to the reality of other people.

Puer aeternus (Latin, "eternal youth"). Indicates a certain type of man who remains too long in adolescent psychology, generally associated with a strong unconscious attachment to the mother (actual or symbolic). Positive traits are spontaneity and openness to change. His female counterpart is the **puella,** an "eternal girl" with a corresponding attachment to the father-world.

Self. The archetype of wholeness and the regulating center of the personality. It is experienced as a transpersonal power which transcends the ego, e.g., God.

Senex (Latin, "old man"). Associated with attitudes that come with advancing age. Negatively, this can mean cynicism, rigidity and extreme conservatism; positive traits are responsibility, orderliness and self-discipline. A well-balanced personality functions appropriately within the puer-senex polarity.

Shadow. An unconscious part of the personality characterized by traits and attitudes, whether negative or positive, which the conscious ego tends to reject or ignore. It is personified in dreams by persons of the same sex as the dreamer. Consciously assimilating one's shadow usually results in an increase of energy.

Symbol. The best possible expression for something essentially unknown. Symbolic thinking is non-linear, right-brain oriented; it is complementary to logical, linear, left-brain thinking.

Transcendent function. The reconciling "third" which emerges from the unconscious (in the form of a symbol or a new attitude) after the conflicting opposites have been consciously differentiated, and the tension between them held.

Transference and countertransference. Particular cases of projection, commonly used to describe the unconscious, emotional bonds that arise between two persons in an analytic or therapeutic relationship.

Uroboros. The mythical snake or dragon that eats its own tail. It is a symbol both for individuation as a self-contained, circular process, and for narcissistic self-absorption.

Index

conflict: 11, 13-14, 27, 29, 59, 62-63,
  65, 88, 95, 97, 99, 101-103
  dreams of, 62-63, 99
coniunctio, 63, 81, 96, 98-99, 104
consciousness: collective, 9-12, 20,
  71, 106, 114-115
  personal (*see also* ego), 9-14, 61
counter-transference, 25, 34, 54-58,
  61, 64, 93, 117

Dai, Bingham, 7
death: 11, 20, 24-25
  in dreams, 25, 41-44, 48-49, 52,
  81-82, 98
depression, 19-20, 41-42, 45-46, 50,
  58-60, 65, 99, 101, 104, 108
diagnosis, through dreams, 26-27,
  38-53, 116
diamond body, 96
dissociation: 15, 30, 45, 72, 102
  in dreams, 52
"dissolve and coagulate," 97
divine marriage, 13
dog, in dreams, 40-45, 47, 52, 94-
  95, 104
dominance/submission pattern, 31,
  44, 53
dream(s): of aborigine, 97-98
  and affect-ego, 61-67
  aggression in, 46-50, 59, 62-63,
  73, 103-104
  and alchemy, 97-100, 117
  of alcohol, 84-86
  of alligator, 47
  amplification of, 13-14, 33-36,
  40, 60, 68-69, 78-79, 100, 103-
  105, 115-116
  of analysand by analyst, 55-58
  of analyst by analysand, 55-56
  anger in, 23, 45-46
  of animals without skin, 50, 59
  and anxiety, 46-50, 52, 101
  archetypal images in, 34-36, 71,
  75-79, 97-100, 115

dream(s) (*cont.*):
  associations (*see also*
  amplification of), 34-36, 68-
  69, 78-79, 87-88
  of automobiles, 83-85
  of baby, 42-45, 52
  of bathrooms, 82
  of birth, 42-44
  of boat, 77-78, 106
  of border crossing, 70-71
  of bridge, 70
  cause and effect, 44
  of civil war, 63
  clairvoyant, 92
  of clothing, 72, 104
  of cockroach, 43-44
  of communion, 30
  as compensation, 23-26, 36-37,
  51, 56, 66-67, 70, 78, 89, 91,
  93-94, 101-104, 107, 116
  and complexes, 15-16, 35, 37, 41-
  44, 52-53, 56, 60-62, 68-79, 82,
  86-87, 110, 116
  of conflict, 62-63, 99
  of *coniunctio,* 63, 81, 98-99, 104
  context, importance of, 34-37,
  50, 68, 80, 83, 86, 116
  control of, 91
  and countertransference, 54-58,
  64
  of death, 25, 41-44, 48-49, 52, 59,
  81-82, 98
  and depression, 59-60, 65, 99,
  101, 108
  details, importance of, 84, 90,
  116
  and diagnosis, 26-27, 38-53, 116
  as disguised reality, 55, 68, 89,
  112
  of dog, 40-45, 47, 52, 94-95, 104
  dramatic structure, 37, 62, 89-90
  of dreaming, 89-90
  of drugs, 84-86
  of the dying, 52, 105

Marie-Louise von Franz, Honorary Patron

Studies in Jungian Psychology
by Jungian Analysts

Limited Edition Paperbacks

MARION WOODMAN (Toronto)
Addiction to Perfection: The Still Unravished Bride. $15
A powerful and authoritative look at the psychology and attitudes of modern women. Illustrated.
The Pregnant Virgin: A Process of Psychological Transformation. $16
A celebration of the feminine, in both men and women, and the search for personal identity. Illus.
The Owl Was a Baker's Daughter: Obesity, Anorexia Nervosa and the Repressed Feminine. $14
Focus on the body as mirror of the psyche in eating disorders and weight disturbances. Illus.

DELDON ANNE MCNEELY (Lynchburg, VA)
Touching: Body Therapy and Depth Psychology. $13
A unique book, showing how these two therapeutic disciplines may be integrated in practice.

JANET O. DALLETT (Seal Harbor, WA)
When the Spirits Come Back. $14
An analyst rediscovers the integrity of the healing process and her own shamanic gifts.

MARIE-LOUISE VON FRANZ (Zurich)
On Divination and Synchronicity: The Psychology of Meaningful Chance. $13
Penetrating study of the irrational and methods of divining fate (Tarot, astrology, I Ching, etc.)
Alchemy: An Introduction to the Symbolism and the Psychology. $18
Invaluable for interpreting images and motifs in modern dreams and drawings. 84 Illustrations.

ALDO CAROTENUTO (Rome)
The Spiral Way: A Woman's Healing Journey. $14
The case history of a 50-year-old woman's Jungian analysis, with focus on dream interpretation.

DARYL SHARP (Toronto)
The Survival Papers: Anatomy of a Midlife Crisis. $15
A powerful presentation of how Jung's major concepts may be experienced in a person's life.

SYLVIA BRINTON PERERA (New York)
Descent to the Goddess: A Way of Initiation for Women. $12
Provocative study of the need for an inner, female authority in a male-oriented society.
The Scapegoat Complex: Mythology of Shadow and Guilt. $13
A hard-hitting exploration of scapegoat psychology, based on mythology and case material.

NANCY QUALLS-CORBETT (Birmingham)
The Sacred Prostitute: Eternal Aspect of the Feminine. $15
Shows how the ancient connection between spirituality and passionate love can be regained. Illus.

Prices and payment in $US (except for Canadian orders)
Please add $1 per book (bookpost) or $3 per book (airmail)
Send check or money order (no Credit Cards)

Write for complete Catalogue

INNER CITY BOOKS
Box 1271, Station Q, Toronto, Canada M4T 2P4